HISTORY OF WESTERN ART IN COMICS

Part Two

From the
Renaissance
to
Modern Art

Marion Augustin

Bruno Heitz

Translated by
George L. Newman

HOLIDAY HOUSE • NEW YORK

To Simon, Andrea, and Rafael
—M.A.

First published in French by Editions Casterman s.a. as L'HISTOIRE DE L'ART EN BD T2.
DE LA RENAISSANCE A NOS JOURS BY MARION AUGUSTIN & BRUNO HEITZ

Library of Congress Cataloging-in-Publication Data

Names: Augustin, Marion, author. | Heitz, Bruno, illustrator. | Newman,
George L., translator. | Augustin, Marion. Histoire de l'art en BD.
De la Renaissance...à l'art moderne.
Title: The history of Western art in comics. From the Renaissance...to
modern art! / Marion Augustin, Bruno Heitz ; translated by George L. Newman.
Other titles: Histoire de l'art en BD. De la Renaissance...à l'art moderne. English
Description: New York City : Holiday House, 2021. | Audience: Ages 10-Up
Audience: Grades 7–9 | Summary: "In this informative graphic novel
sequel, two kids and their grandpa continue their adventurous guided
exploration of art and civilization beginning with the Renaissance and
moving forward into modern art"—Provided by publisher.
Identifiers: LCCN 2021010440 | ISBN 9780823446476 (hardcover)
ISBN 9780823446483 (paperback)
Subjects: LCSH: Art, Modern—Juvenile literature. | Art, Modern—Comic books, strips, etc.
Classification: LCC N6350 .A9413 2021 | DDC 709.04—dc23
LC record available at https://lccn.loc.gov/2021010440

ISBN: 978-0-8234-4647-6 (hardcover)
ISBN: 978-0-8234-4648-3 (paperback)

Reproduction credits

Certain major twentieth-century artists are not mentioned or represented in this book,
and others are mentioned very little considering the importance of their work.
This is due to the difficulty or impossibility of obtaining the rights to draw or reproduce their works.

74: *Woman with a Hat* (1905) by Henri Matisse, with the gracious permission of Héritiers Matisse; 77: *Les Demoiselles d'Avignon* (1907) by Pablo Picasso © Succession Picasso 2017 / Oil on canvas (96 x 92 in), acquired with the help of The Lillie P. Bliss Bequest. 333.1939 © 2017. Digital image, The Museum of Modern Art, New York / Scala, Florence; eBook distribution © 2021 Estate of Pablo Picasso / Artists Rights Society (ARS), New York; 78: *Fruit Dish, Ace of Clubs* (1913) by Georges Braque © SABAM Belgium 2017; 79: *Fountain* (1917) and *Bicycle Wheel* (1913) by Marcel Duchamp © Succession Marcel Duchamp / SABAM Belgium 2017; 80: *The Song of Love* (1914) by Giorgio de Chirico © SABAM Belgium 2017; 81a: *The Persistence of Memory* (1931) by Salvador Dali © Fundació Gala - Salvador Dali / SABAM Belgium 2017; 81b: *The Treachery of Images* (1929) by René Magritte © Ch. Herscovici - SABAM Belgium 2017; 83a: *Ohhh ... Alright* (1964) by Roy Lichtenstein © SABAM Belgium 2017; 83b: *Four Marilyns* (c. 1964) by Andy Warhol © The Andy Warhol Foundation for the Visual Arts, Inc. / SABAM Belgium 2017; Marilyn Monroe (TM); Rights of Publicity and Persona Rights: The Estate of Marilyn Monroe LLC. marilynmonroe.com; 84a: *Maman* (1999) by Louise Bourgeois © Louise Bourgeois Trust / SABAM Belgium 2017; 84b: *Three Figures in a Room* (1964) by Francis Bacon © SABAM Belgium 2017; 86a: *The Last Supper* (1498) by Leonardo da Vinci © Haltadefinizione / Italian Ministry of Culture / Wikimedia Commons; 86b: *Moses* (1513) by Michelangelo © Archives Casterman; 86c: *Portrait of Baldassare Castiglione* (1514–1515) by Raphael Sanzio © Elsa Lambert / C2RMF / Wikimedia Commons; 87a: *The Tempest* (c. 1507) by Giorgione © Galerie de l'Académie, Venice / Wikimedia Commons; 87b: *Portrait of the Artist Holding a Thistle* (1493) by Albrecht Dürer © Museo del Prado / Wikimedia Commons; 87c: *The Garden of Earthly Delights* (1494–1505) by Hieronymus Bosch © Museo del Prado / Wikimedia Commons; 88a: *The Judgement of Paris* (1632–1635) by Peter Paul Rubens © Archives Casterman ; 88b: *Las Meninas* (1656) by Diego Velázquez © Galeriaonline / Museo del Prado / Wikimedia Commons ; 89a: *Apollo and Daphne* (1622–1625) by Bernin © Gaspar Alves / Wikimedia Commons; 89b: *David with the Head of Goliath* (1606–1607) by Caravaggio ©Lafit86 / Galleria Borghese / Wikimedia Commons; 89c: *Girl with a Pearl Earring* (1665) by Johannes Vermeer © Archives Casterman; 89d: *Self Portrait as the Apostle Paul* (1661) by Rembrandt Van Rijn © Michel Pierre, Archives Casterman; 90a: *Pilgrimage to the Isle of Cythera* (1717) by Antoine Watteau © Musée du Louvre / J.-M. Coblence; 90b: *The Parasol* (1777) by Francisco de Goya © Museo del Prado / Wikimedia Commons; 90c: *Portrait of Louis-François Bertin* (1832) by Jean-Auguste-Dominique Ingres © Musée du Louvre / J.-M. Coblence; 91a: *The Raft of the Medusa* (1819) by Théodore Géricault © Musée du Louvre / Archives Casterman; 91b: *The Balcony* (1868) by Edouard Manet © Google Art Project / Wikimedia Commons; 91c: *The Thinker* (1917) by Auguste Rodin © Google Art Project / Wikimedia Commons; 92a: *Dance at Moulin de la Galette* (1876) by Auguste Renoir © Allart / Musée d'Orsay / Wikimedia Commons; 92b: *La Montagne Sainte-Victoire* (1885–1905) by Paul Cézanne © Archives Casterman; 92c: *Self-Portrait* (1889) by Vincent Van Gogh © Musée d'Orsay / J.-M. Coblence; 93a: *Composition VII* (1913) by Wassily Kandinsky © Galerie Tretiakov Moscow / Wikimedia Commons; 93b: *Composition in Red, Yellow, Blue, and Black* (1921) by Piet Mondrian © Gemeentemuseum Den Haag / Wikimedia Commons.

Art is everywhere in our lives: in the shapes of
houses and monuments, on posters glued to walls,
in films. But where did it come from? Why have
people felt the need to produce works of art? What
artists have influenced the history of art? What
materials have they used? What techniques? How
have artworks been passed from one civilization
to another, from one artist to another? Why have
some been preserved and others forgotten?

This second volume traces the links between the
principal artistic movements and artists in the West
from the Renaissance to our time. It is primarily
devoted to the visual arts of painting and sculpture,
but also to installations and street art.

Turn the page to relive the fabulous history of art
through the ages—treasures of the imagination,
marvels of creativity, surprises, and thrills await.

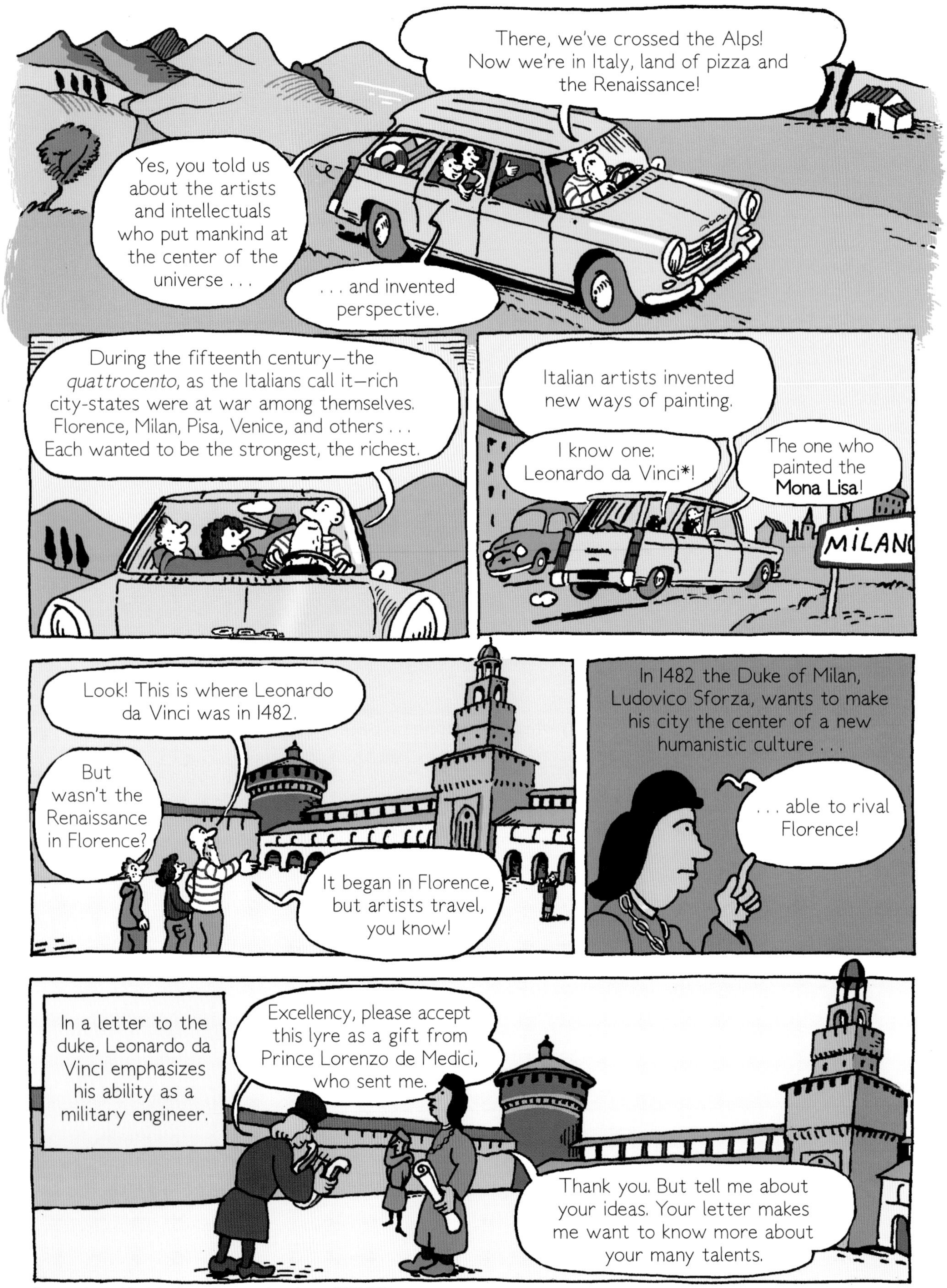
There, we've crossed the Alps! Now we're in Italy, land of pizza and the Renaissance!
Yes, you told us about the artists and intellectuals who put mankind at the center of the universe . . .
. . . and invented perspective.
During the fifteenth century—the *quattrocento*, as the Italians call it—rich city-states were at war among themselves. Florence, Milan, Pisa, Venice, and others . . . Each wanted to be the strongest, the richest.
Italian artists invented new ways of painting.
I know one: Leonardo da Vinci*!
The one who painted the **Mona Lisa**!
MILAN
Look! This is where Leonardo da Vinci was in 1482.
But wasn't the Renaissance in Florence?
It began in Florence, but artists travel, you know!
In 1482 the Duke of Milan, Ludovico Sforza, wants to make his city the center of a new humanistic culture . . .
. . . able to rival Florence!
In a letter to the duke, Leonardo da Vinci emphasizes his ability as a military engineer.
Excellency, please accept this lyre as a gift from Prince Lorenzo de Medici, who sent me.
Thank you. But tell me about your ideas. Your letter makes me want to know more about your many talents.

*Leonardo da Vinci, Italian painter and engineer (1452-1519)

Excellency, this cannon can sow terror among your enemies. When the shell explodes, it sprays shot in all directions.

Fascinating! I've never seen anything like it.

Very useful for the wars that are coming.

Leonardo becomes the duke's official artist and engineer. He stays in Milan for 17 years.

I want to understand the laws that govern the world we live in.

Leonardo, this is the dome designed by the architect Bramante.* I want you to decorate the church too.

I gladly accept this honor.

Master da Vinci hasn't finished, Excellency, and—

What a marvel! The apostles are so alive, in the middle of a discussion, stunned by Christ's words!

Leonardo paints **The Last Supper** in the refectory of Santa Maria delle Grazie. He uses perspective to emphasize the drama of the scene. Everything is organized around Jesus, and backlit by a sunny landscape.

Excellency, each face shows a different emotion. I'm constantly looking for models. For Judas I need the face of a scoundrel, because he is going to betray Jesus!

*Donato Bramante, Italian architect (1444-1514)

Leonardo da Vinci studies the human body in order to understand its internal functions as well as its external appearance. His goal: to be able to draw it perfectly.

Here's the heart. . . .

And there are the lungs.

He also wants to write a treatise on anatomy. In the process, he makes important discoveries.

So the heart, located on the left, is like a pump that sends the blood through the arteries.

And the soul?

In 1499, after several attempts, the army of King Louis XII of France captures Milan. Duke Sforza is forced to flee.

Leonardo da Vinci leaves Milan to look elsewhere for patrons.

Farewell, Milan . . .

I'm going home to Florence.

In Flanders, in Northern Europe, there is a growing taste for painted portraits, and the Italians follow the Flemish. First the nobles and then the rich merchants commission their own portraits. In 1503, Francesco del Giocondo pays a visit to Leonardo.

I want to commission a portrait of my beloved wife, Lisa Gherardini, for our new home.

A private portrait . . . why not?

If the money's good . . .

For Leonardo, the planning is more important than the execution. Before he begins a painting, he does a lot of research, makes sketches . . . He loves these studies.

Leonardo adopts innovations from Northern Europe: the landscape in the background, the three-quarter pose of the model, the prominently visible hands.

Mona Lisa's eyes seem to look past the viewer. She is very much present, and at the same time distant.

Leonardo invents the "sfumato" technique: contours are lightly blurred, softening the lines and giving a hazy effect. He achieves it by applying multiple ultra-thin layers of glaze.

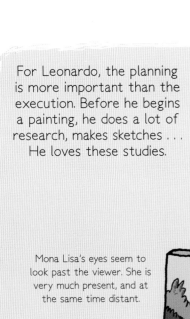

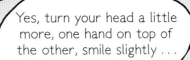

Yes, turn your head a little more, one hand on top of the other, smile slightly . . .

Your Mona Lisa isn't all that pretty.

But everyone knows her. Why is that?

La Gioconda fascinates people. Is it her smile? A mystery!

Leonardo was never paid for the painting, which he kept for the rest of his life. When he died in France in 1519, King Francis I purchased it. Today people come from all over the world to see it in the Louvre museum.

In 1503, the leaders of Florence decide to renovate and decorate the town hall—the Palazzo Vecchio, or Old Palace—to show their power and celebrate their military victories. They call on Leonardo da Vinci and a young sculptor who is already highly renowned: Michelangelo Buonarroti*. The competition between these two masters is intense.

So, Leonardo, your fresco of the Battle of Anghiari isn't going very fast. Are you ever going to finish it?

What a jerk! I hate him!

Just keep working on your Battle of Cascina! We'll see who's better at painting the fury of combat!

A promising young artist who learns a lot from his contact with these two geniuses is Raffaello Sanzio, known as Raphael.

For my painting I'll apply what I learned from Leonardo: the figures are in motion, exchanging looks that link them with one another, and grouped in a triangle.

Michelangelo and Leonardo never complete their frescoes in the Palazzo Vecchio, and the paintings are now lost. In 1505, Michelangelo is summoned to Rome to work for Pope Julius II.

Leonardo remains in Florence, lonely and bitter.

All the artists worthy of the name are going to Rome! That blockhead Michelangelo and young Raphael.

. . . What about me? What patron is going to give me any work?

*Michelangelo Buonarroti, Italian painter and sculptor (1475-1564)

Pope Julius II strives to increase Rome's glory . . . and his own. He admires Michelangelo's **Pietà** (a sculpture of the Virgin Mary mourning her dead son, Jesus).

For my tomb I want a work as marvelous as your **Pietà**!

For you, I shall seek out the most flawless marble.

Like Leonardo, Michelangelo studies anatomy to better portray the human body. He is inspired by ancient statues, but he adds the expression of feelings.

Moses, I can see you in this block of marble!

I shall release you from the stone and make you live!

The pope decides to rebuild the basilica of Saint Peter in Rome. The architect Bramante presents plans for a huge building in the shape of a Greek cross.

Look, Excellency! A circle in a square, a symbol of eternity.

The first stone is laid in 1506. The work will continue for several centuries.

I want Rome to have the greatest church in Christendom.

In Rome, many ancient statues are unearthed during construction work. They have an influence on many artists.

What beauty—and at the same time what suffering!

Yes, look how the bodies are twisted in all directions. . . .

Work on the nearby Basilica of Saint Peter has cracked the vault of the Sistine Chapel. The pope asks Michelangelo to repair the vault and then decorate it.

Michelangelo, I want a new vault for the chapel built by my uncle, Pope Sixtus.

You'll find a way!

But Your Excellency, I'm a sculptor. . . .

Michelangelo works on the high ceiling of the chapel in sections, separated by trompe-l'oeil elements inspired by Greek architecture. The nine central scenes are taken from Genesis, the first book of the Bible, and include God's creation of the world, then the creation of the first man, and finally the story of Noah.

Send up more lime!

Master, tomorrow we'll need to move the scaffolding so we can celebrate Mass.

Between 1508 and 1512, Michelangelo paints more than 300 figures on the vault. Their bodies are powerful, but their gestures are delicate.

The scene showing God's creation of Adam is undoubtedly one of the best-known images in the world. In the center of the vault, God has just created a man in his image. By touching him with a finger, he has instilled life.

These nudes in a church, though . . .

Michelangelo is inspired by God to paint this way.

Sublime!

Michelangelo shows sibyls, women in ancient mythology who could predict the future. Their feet barely touch the ground.

Michelangelo's fame is immense. Some artists have portraits of him; others are inspired by his works.

I would so love to be as good as you, Master.

At the age of seventy, Michelangelo becomes one of the architects of Saint Peter's in Rome.

The dome is almost finished. Just as well, because I'm feeling pretty old.

Beginning in 1509, with the support of Bramante, who is also from the city of Urbino, Raphael* is chosen to help decorate the living quarters of Pope Julius II in Rome. After a few months, all the other artists withdraw and the job is left to Raphael.

I have to decorate the pope's apartments by myself! And it has to be as beautiful as Michelangelo's Sistine ceiling!

You can handle it, master.

We'll back you up.

For the pope's library, Raphael gets advice from intellectuals in the pope's circle.

A synthesis of human thought and Christian faith. Poetry, theology, philosophy . . . this is a magnificent project!

Beyond that, the painter has complete freedom to create the work.

An homage to the Greek scholars. . . . You've given me an idea, Master Bembo!

In the library, every wall is covered with frescoes. The best-known fresco brings together the great thinkers of antiquity: **The School of Athens**, an imaginary scene of an academy open to all scholars. In its composition, with figures spread out in small groups, this fresco exemplifies the new work of the Renaissance.

What a magnificent scene! Faith and knowledge, together, lead to truth. Aristotle and Plato are in the center. . . .

Here's Pythagoras, busy studying.

That's Heraclitus.

Yes, with Michelangelo's face!

*Raffaello Sanzio, known as Raphael, Italian painter (1483-1520)

The frescoes in the pope's apartments are an immediate success. Raphael is at the height of his art, recognized for his draftsmanship, his color, and his composition.

What an honor to make your portrait! I shall try to paint the respect I have for you.

Men pass away, Raphael. . . . I will be remembered because I allowed Raphael and Michelangelo to express their talent.

Eminent people, nobles and clergymen, come to Raphael to commission their portraits. The painter finds himself in charge of a real business, with dozens of assistants.

Do you have the drawing for the Duke of Urbino's portrait?

And for the Madonna, should I still use blue?

Talk to Giulio.

The pope's banker, Agostino Chigi, builds the Villa Farnesina near Rome. There, in 1513, Raphael paints **The Triumph of Galatea**. The dynamic composition of the fresco, with all of the figures moving in different directions, shows his virtuosity.

Who is the model for your sublime Galatea?

No one in particular. I paint from a certain idea in my mind.

Raphael revolutionizes painting and the role of the artist in society.

In the sixteenth century, Italy was in a permanent state of war: Rome against Naples, Milan against Venice. . . . In 1527, mutinous troops of Holy Roman Emperor Charles V besieged Rome, captured the city, pillaged its riches, and killed thousands of its people.

That's awful!

Goodbye, Rome. . . .

We're off to Venice.

During all those years of Roman glory, Venice also attracted exceptional artists.

Saint Mark's Square!

The Grand Canal!

VE 722

Painters like Giovanni Bellini* introduce new techniques, mixing Byzantine, Italian, and Flemish influences.

Vittore*, I've had enough of wood. Canvas is better! It resists the dampness here in Venice.

And it's easier to carry.

Slow-drying oil is better for painting details and the reflections of light on the water of the lagoon.

In Venice there are *scuole*—schools, which are sometimes very rich—that commission works to show their prestige.

Vittore Carpaccio, we want to honor Saint Jerome with your paintings, which are so true to life!

*Giovanni Bellini, Italian painter (1430-1516)
*Vittore Carpaccio, Italian painter (c. 1460-1525)

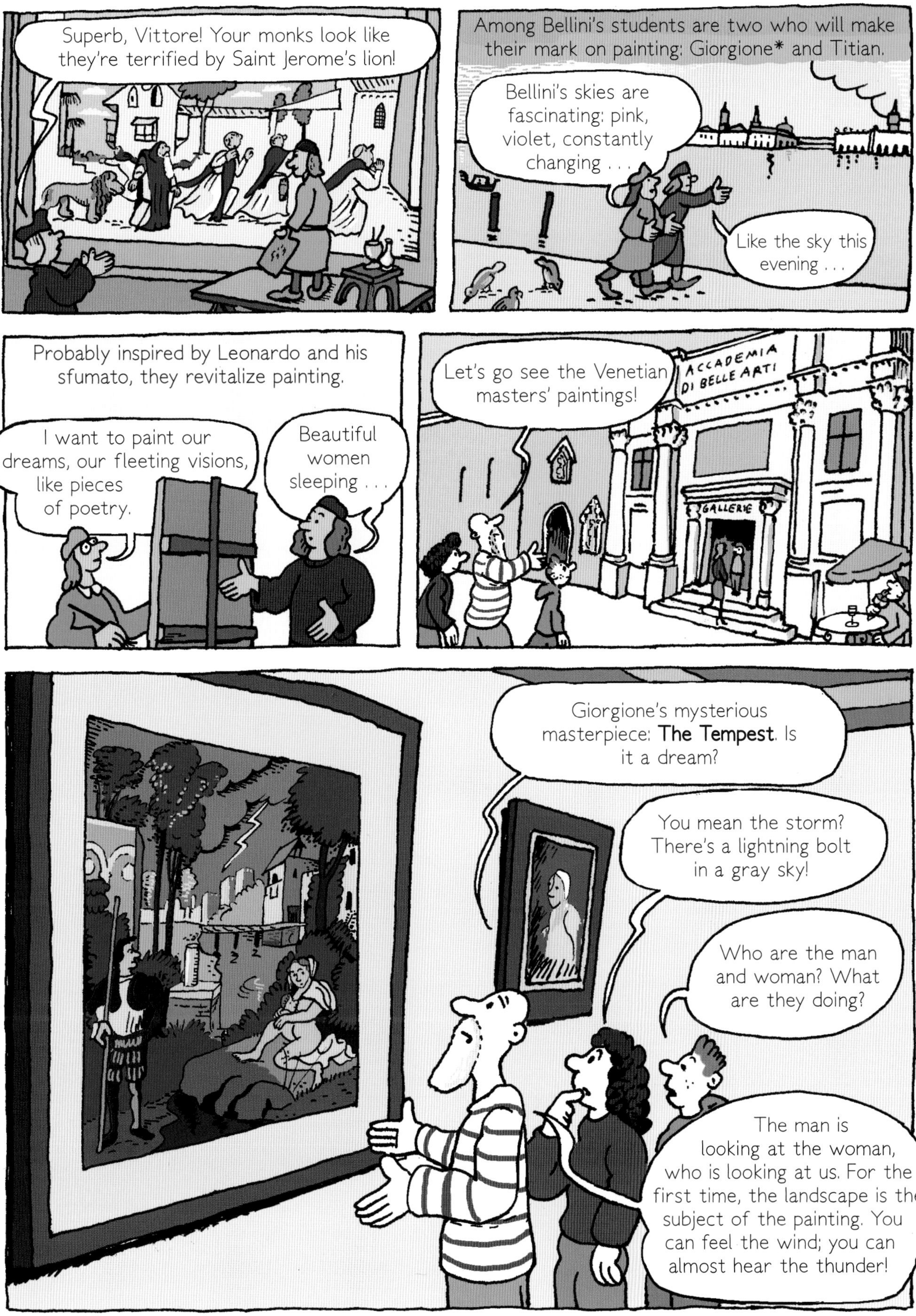
Superb, Vittore! Your monks look like they're terrified by Saint Jerome's lion!
Among Bellini's students are two who will make their mark on painting: Giorgione* and Titian.
Bellini's skies are fascinating: pink, violet, constantly changing . . .
Like the sky this evening . . .
Probably inspired by Leonardo and his sfumato, they revitalize painting.
I want to paint our dreams, our fleeting visions, like pieces of poetry.
Beautiful women sleeping . . .
Let's go see the Venetian masters' paintings!
ACCADEMIA DI BELLE ARTI
GALLERIE
Giorgione's mysterious masterpiece: **The Tempest**. Is it a dream?
You mean the storm? There's a lightning bolt in a gray sky!
Who are the man and woman? What are they doing?
The man is looking at the woman, who is looking at us. For the first time, the landscape is the subject of the painting. You can feel the wind; you can almost hear the thunder!

*Giorgione da Castelfranco, Italian painter (c. 1477-1511)

When Giovanni Bellini dies, in 1516, Titian* is named the official painter of the Republic of Venice. He establishes a studio on the Grand Canal.

Your next commission?

Yes, the Franciscans have asked me for an altarpiece for their church.

It's gigantic! Can we see it?

Patience! After it's installed.

On May 19, 1518, the **Assumption of the Virgin** altarpiece is installed in the church of Santa Maria dei Frari. The huge painting is revolutionary: it bursts with color and movement, unlike the usual religious paintings. The Virgin Mary is lively, joyous, surrounded by adoring angels.

They're all in motion. . . .

All that movement, it's unbelievable.

The apostles at the bottom are in shadow. Mary is in the light of God. . . .

What lightness!

What reds!

The Venetians are won over by such flamboyance. From then on, Titian is unrivaled, and he receives more commissions. He organizes his studio like a business, with numerous employees. But following the practice of the time, he alone signs the works.

*Tiziano Vecelli, known as Titian, Italian painter (1490-1576)

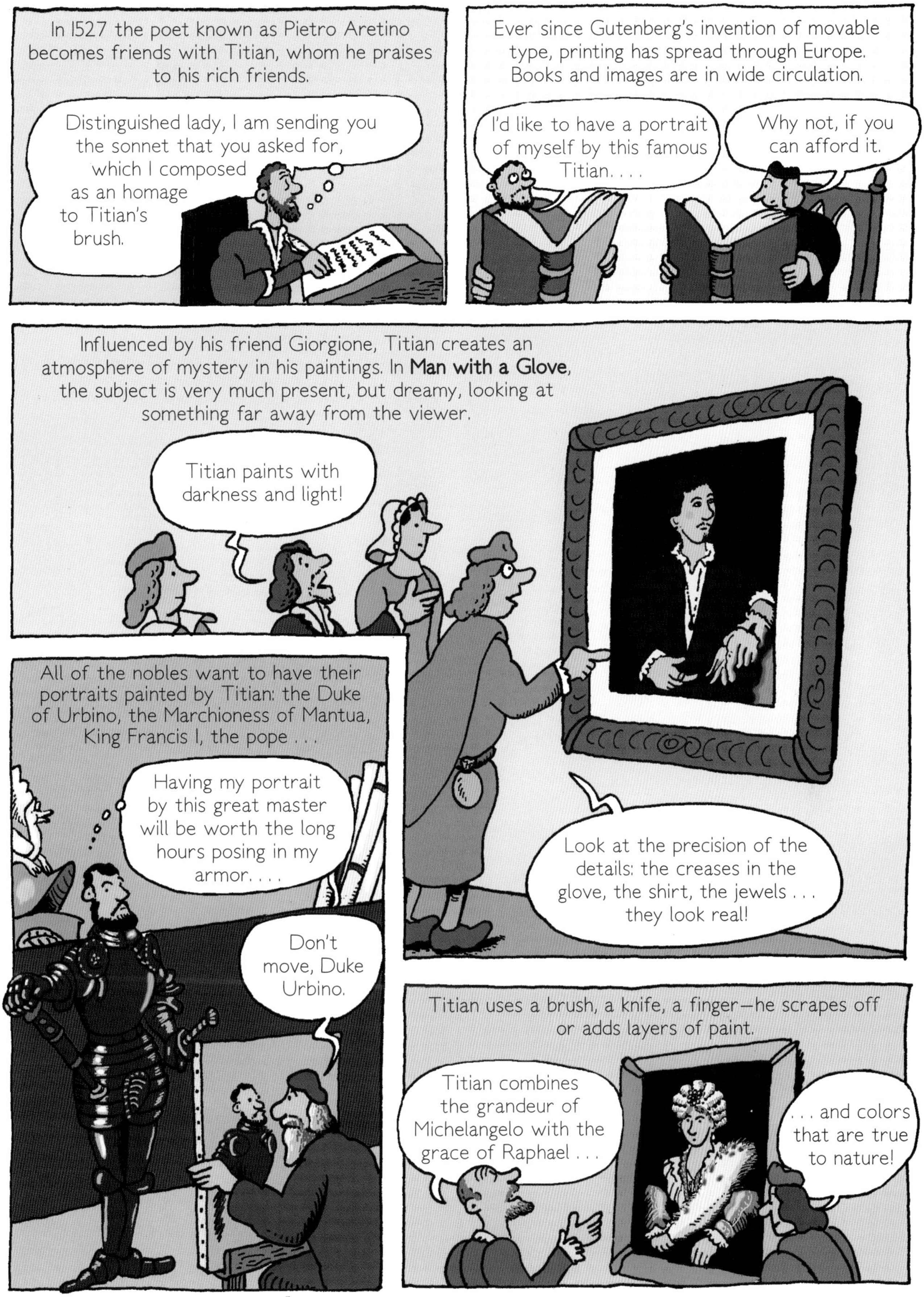
In 1527 the poet known as Pietro Aretino becomes friends with Titian, whom he praises to his rich friends.
Distinguished lady, I am sending you the sonnet that you asked for, which I composed as an homage to Titian's brush.
Ever since Gutenberg's invention of movable type, printing has spread through Europe. Books and images are in wide circulation.
I'd like to have a portrait of myself by this famous Titian. . . .
Why not, if you can afford it.
Influenced by his friend Giorgione, Titian creates an atmosphere of mystery in his paintings. In **Man with a Glove**, the subject is very much present, but dreamy, looking at something far away from the viewer.
Titian paints with darkness and light!
Look at the precision of the details: the creases in the glove, the shirt, the jewels . . . they look real!
All of the nobles want to have their portraits painted by Titian: the Duke of Urbino, the Marchioness of Mantua, King Francis I, the pope . . .
Having my portrait by this great master will be worth the long hours posing in my armor. . . .
Don't move, Duke Urbino.
Titian uses a brush, a knife, a finger—he scrapes off or adds layers of paint.
Titian combines the grandeur of Michelangelo with the grace of Raphael . . .
. . . and colors that are true to nature!

Besides their portraits, Titian's rich clients like works that feature the heroes of mythology.

Master Titian, I want to give my young wife a painting. Something to inspire love . . .

Love . . . Venus. . . . I remember Giorgione's painting of a beautiful woman sleeping. . . .

The nude woman that Titian paints in **Venus of Urbino** is wide awake and looking at the observer. Lying on a bed, she calmly invites the viewer's gaze. Titian shows her in a palace. She is no longer a goddess, but a young woman proud of her beauty.

The artist uses glazes to give her skin a velvety look.

Colors in rich, subtle shades are applied in very thin, almost transparent layers.

This painting will fascinate and inspire many other artists.

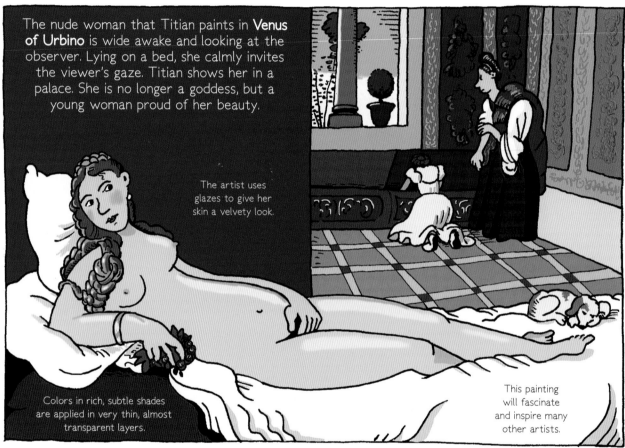

In 1530, Titian is presented to the powerful Charles V. They develop a mutual respect, and Titian is appointed official painter of the Holy Roman Emperor.

This is Master Titian from Venice.

Word of your talent precedes you. Welcome to my court. I would like a portrait. . . .

It is an honor.

In 1548, Charles V is at the height of his political power, and wants to immortalize his victory at the Battle of Mühlberg.

The emperor summons me to Augsburg, and I can't refuse. Francesco, you're coming with me.

Master Titian, I can give you two hours, no more.

I shall do my best, Your Majesty.

This first royal equestrian portrait begins a tradition that will be followed by the painters Van Dyck, Velazquez, and Rubens.

Remember the advisers' instructions: celebrate the victory, show Charles's power, his strength in his armor . . .

The emperor is courageous and he will triumph, but he is alone, terribly alone. . . .

In **Charles V at Mühlberg**, the emperor is not shown in the heat of combat, or after his victory, but riding alone to the battle.

At the end of his life, Titian's paintings become darker and darker. More than a likeness, he tries to portray his own feelings. He dies at the age of 86, honored as an equal of the greatest princes.

It's finished? But . . . you can see the brushstrokes. . . .

Yes, Horacio. The details aren't important. Truth is in the color—that's what painting is.

What's that palace?

That was a German warehouse in the fifteenth and sixteenth centuries. Merchants from Germany met and stored their goods there. Artists also stopped there.

Like many other artists from Northern Europe, Albrecht Dürer* is drawn to Venice.

What light! What colors!

The trip gives painters the chance to study relics of antiquity as well as treasures of the early Renaissance.

To become a great painter one must tirelessly copy the works of the masters!

Back in Germany, young Dürer writes a treatise on perspective.

I'm trying to discover mathematical rules for the ideal beauty created by God.

I'll engrave it all on wood so it can be printed and distributed.

At the end of the fifteenth century, Nuremberg is an intellectual center where printing thrives. Images from woodcuts are reproduced on paper and widely distributed. It's a real revolution.

The artist engraves a wooden plate using gouges. He removes everything that will be left white in the print

The plate is inked; the ink goes only on the uncut surfaces.

The plate is put into a press with a sheet of paper, and the paper is printed.

*Albrecht Dürer, German painter and engraver (1471-1528)

Dürer, a virtuoso draftsman, has a passion for engraving. He creates images illustrating the Book of Revelation.

Look, here are the horsemen of the Apocalypse!

They're frightening!

Dürer assembles his 15 plates and publishes the collection himself. The success is immediate.

No more need to look for a patron! I can make a good living and travel. What freedom!

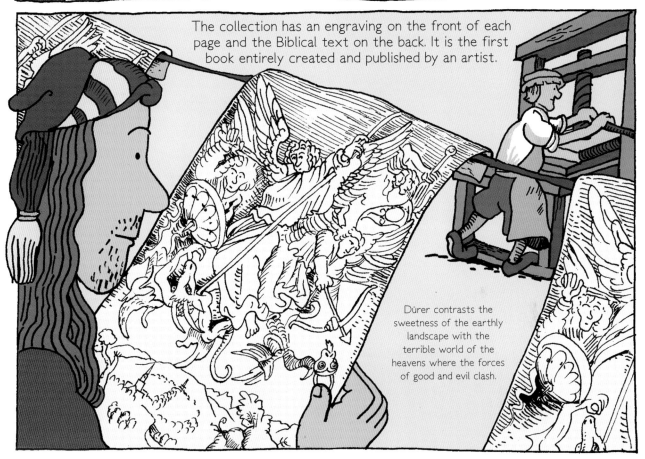

The collection has an engraving on the front of each page and the Biblical text on the back. It is the first book entirely created and published by an artist.

Dürer contrasts the sweetness of the earthly landscape with the terrible world of the heavens where the forces of good and evil clash.

Such success breeds envy! Dürer's engravings are copied all over Europe.

Here's a copy by the Italian Raimondi.

Well, let him copy! My engravings will bear my monogram.

Dürer turns his signature into a "brand" that quickly becomes famous.

In Italy, Dürer saw how artists were much more highly regarded than they were in Germany. He wants to show that he is the equal of Nuremberg's powerful people.

I'll paint my portrait to show them who I am! Not an artisan, or a tradesman, but a rich man like them!

Unlike the usual portraits, in this self-portrait Dürer paints himself facing the observer with his hand raised to his chest, a pose usually reserved for pictures of Christ.

You're not dressed like a painter, you're not holding any tools, and you're wearing an expensive coat.

Dürer takes an interest in everything: plants, animals . . . His watercolor painting of a hare is still popular today.

Observe nature, let it guide you, and don't stray from it.

During the same period, in Wittenberg in northern Germany, the monk Martin Luther posts **95 Theses** on the doors of the church, denouncing the behavior of the pope in Rome.

The indulgences issued by Pope Julius II turn believers away from the faith. We must return to the Bible!

Yes! One doesn't trade the health of one's soul for money, not even for money to build the church of Saint Peter in Rome!

Thanks to the printing press, Luther's Theses are disseminated quickly. The Reformation is opposed to the abuses of the Catholic Church. Its supporters are called "Protestants." The clergy reacts strongly; it's the beginning of a long battle that will engulf all of Europe.

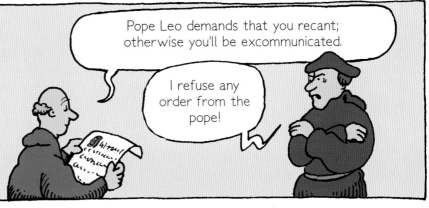

Pope Leo demands that you recant; otherwise you'll be excommunicated.

I refuse any order from the pope!

Luther's supporters disagree with Catholics on how to save their souls and enter into paradise.

Only the believer's faith and God's grace can open the gates of Paradise!

For Luther, images distract the believer from his faith. Highly decorated churches are targeted by the Protestants.

This battle plays a decisive role in the evolution of European art. In the north, the Protestants are more and more numerous.

Here in the Low Countries there are no more commissions from the Catholic Church. What can we do?

Portraits?

Some painters are followers of the Reformation. One is the German Lucas Cranach*, who trained in Albrecht Dürer's studio. He becomes friends with Luther.

Not too many bright colors. Keep it simple, Lucas!

I'll make the composition very plain, my dear Martin.

*Lucas Cranach, German painter (1472-1553)

After working in Vienna, Lucas Cranach leaves for Wittenberg and is appointed official painter of the princes of Saxony. His renown grows, and he establishes a studio along with his two sons, Hans and Lucas the Younger. He paints many nudes inspired by ancient mythology, the Bible, and medieval legends.

Another Venus?

Yes, but look at the typically German landscape, with a Gothic village reflected in the water. . . . And don't forget that my Venuses are a warning against the temptations of the flesh.

Venus has almond-shaped eyes, the body of an adolescent, and very white skin.

She is dressed in a stylish hat and jewels.

Paintings of idealized nudes are very popular in Germany. Behind their sensuality, there is always a moralistic message.

Besides Venuses, Cranach paints portraits of many eminent people of his time, both Protestants and Catholics.

This is my portrait of Erasmus of Rotterdam, the prince of humanism.

But Master, you've never seen him!

Cranach's portrait of the great philosopher Erasmus is based on a portrait by the German Hans Holbein the Younger*. Did Cranach see the painting? Or an engraving?

The Renaissance travels—to Germany and Italy, but also to the Low Countries, England, and France. In 1526, Hans Holbein the Younger flees the Reformation to seek his fortune in England. Erasmus recommends him to friends close to King Henry VIII.

My dear Sir Thomas, I can make a portrait of your large family. . . .

*Hans Holbein the Younger, German painter (1497-1543)

Holbein specializes in portraits of merchants, clergymen, and diplomats living in London. His talent for painting materials, details, and the character of his subjects is quickly recognized.

I want to show my future wife what a prosperous and respected man I am.

It will all be there: your age, your profession, your wealth . . . and more!

In 1534, thanks to his large painting **The Ambassadors**, Holbein is named the official painter of King Henry VIII. In this masterpiece, he makes a double portrait showing the friendship and compatibility of the two subjects.

And in front, by your feet, I'll paint an anamorphosis.

A what?

Signs of wealth are everywhere: the floor mosaic, a Turkish rug, furs, jewels . . .

The shelves are crowded with things that evoke scholarly activities: scientific devices, books, musical instruments . . .

An anamorphosis is an optical distortion in which a figure appears or disappears depending on the angle from which it is viewed.

Yes! They're rich . . . but there's a "memento mori"*: Salvation comes only through faith.

Horrors! A grinning skull!

*a reminder of mortality

Holbein and his assistants paint numerous portraits of King Henry VIII. Cultured and close to the humanists, the sovereign nevertheless rules in an authoritarian manner, as a despot.

> I want him to take up all the space in the picture.

> Master Holbein, in a few centuries your vision of King Henry will be the one that people remember.

The king's piercing gaze is turned toward the viewer.

His embroidered and bejeweled clothes stand out against the monochrome background.

> I hope he likes it. Otherwise . . . it's curtains!

Throughout Europe, the religious conflict becomes more violent. Even before the Reformation, the Dutch Hieronymus Bosch* depicted the struggle between good and evil in his triptych **The Last Judgment**.

> Demons, monsters, witches, somewhere between humans and beasts . . .

> What a nightmare!

> Only faith can save us from hell!

Bosch's creatures can be part human, part plant, part animal. . . .

> An unbounded imagination to terrify sinners!

> Stop! You're scaring me!

*Hieronymus Bosch, Dutch painter (c. 1450–1516)

Pieter Brueghel* is a painter in the Catholic south of the Low Countries. Like Hieronymus Bosch, he is inspired by popular proverbs.

In contrast to the prevailing Renaissance taste, Brueghel doesn't try to paint ideal beauty.

I paint the living men and women that I see.

Brueghel is the first artist to show peasants realistically, in their work and their amusements. These new artworks, which are not portraits or historical or religious scenes, are called "genre paintings."

In this bird's-eye view, the observer is above the scene. All of the people are in motion. Each part of scene is linked to another.

The Holy Family has just arrived in Bethlehem for the census.

It takes a good eye to spot Mary, Joseph, and Jesus . . .

THE CENSUS AT BETHLEHEM, 1566

The title refers to the Bible story, but the scene shows a Flemish village of the sixteenth century. Unlike in works from the Middle Ages, the religious figures are not made to stand out either by their size or by having golden haloes.

*Pieter Brueghel, Flemish painter (1525-1569)

In France, too, the Renaissance arrives at the beginning of the sixteenth century. Francis I, impressed by the splendors he saw in Italy, brings Italian artists to France. In 1516, Leonardo da Vinci joins his new patron in the Loire Valley.

For Chambord I'm thinking about a double spiral stair: people could go up and down without meeting.

A double helix . . . splendid, Master!

At Chambord, Francis I wants to build a palace that resembles an ancient fortress, but in the Italian style. This huge project will take 30 years and require 240,000 tons of stone!

The slate roofs recall castles and cathedrals; 300 chimneys accent the roofline.

The chateau has a central keep, "Italian style" roof terraces, and loggias.

It retains the structure of a fortress, but now the massive towers are pierced by windows.

The surrounding gardens are laid out geometrically.

Nothing great is ever accomplished without passion!

It's an expensive passion, sire.

In 1539, Francis I receives his rival Charles V at Chambord. The work is still not finished, but the emperor is impressed.

Chambord is a model of human enterprise!

Francis I undertakes the renovation of the Fontainebleau Palace, which he wants to make the seat of his government. The site becomes a hotbed of creativity. The Italians Rosso Fiorentino* and Francesco Primaticcio* are invited to come.

Instead of a passage open to the weather, I propose to build a gallery . . . like in Rome.

The king's gallery . . .

The gallery of Francis I is built and decorated between 1530 and 1539. The paintings show idealized princes: Francis I and his model, Alexander the Great.

Paintings, paneling, stucco, frescoes—from floor to ceiling, every surface is richly decorated.

The emblems of the king are everywhere.

With this decoration, Master Rosso, you have contributed to the flowering of the Renaissance in France!

The artistic influences that flow from the project become known as the "Fontainebleau School."

*Giovanni Battista di Jacopo, known as Rosso Fiorentino, Italian painter (1494-1540)
*Francesco Primaticcio, Italian painter (1504-1570)

Time Line of the Renaissance and the Modern Era

1492 Lorenzo de Medici dies in Florence.
Christopher Columbus discovers America.

1498 Vasco da Gama reaches India.

1508 Michelangelo begins his frescoes at the
Sistine Chapel in Rome.

1515 After his victory at the Battle of Marignano,
Francis I occupies Milan.

1517 In Germany, Martin Luther posts his *95 Theses*
criticizing the Catholic Church.

1519 Leonardo da Vinci dies in Amboise, France.

1520 Magellan sets out to sail around the world.

1527 Charles V's troops sack Rome.

1534 King Henry VIII becomes head of the Church of England.

1540 Pope Paul III approves the formation of the Jesuit Order.

1542 The tribunals of the Roman Inquisition
are created by the pope.

1545-1563 The Council of Trent discusses reform
of the Catholic Church.

1552 The Peace of Augsburg is signed in Germany
by Charles V and the Protestant princes.

1566 Iconoclasts attack Catholic churches in the Low Countries.

1562-1598 French Catholics and Protestants engage in the Wars of Religion.

1579 In the Low Countries, the Protestant north separates from the south and becomes the United Provinces of the Netherlands.

1598 The Edict of Nantes ends the Wars of Religion in France.

1610 Galileo observes the planets with his telescope and confirms that the earth revolves around the sun.

1648 The Royal Academy of Painting is created in Paris.

1661-1715 Louis XIV reigns as king of France.

1684 The Hall of Mirrors at Versailles is inaugurated.

1688 In England, King James II is deposed in the "Glorious Revolution."

1751 The Encyclopédie, edited by Diderot and d'Alembert, is published.

1783 The United States of America wins independence.

1789 The French Revolution begins.

1798 Napoleon Bonaparte begins his expedition to Egypt.

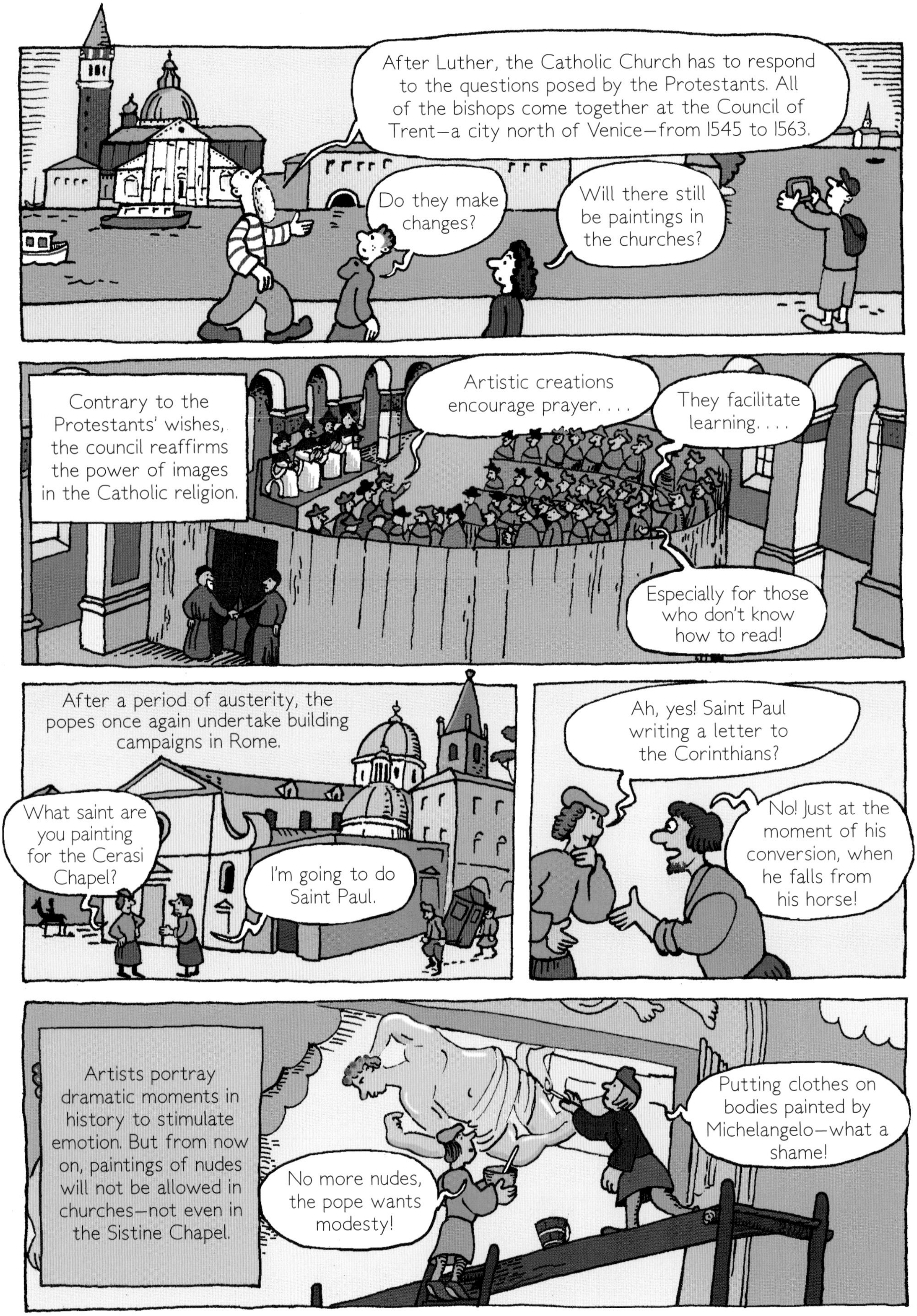

After Luther, the Catholic Church has to respond to the questions posed by the Protestants. All of the bishops come together at the Council of Trent—a city north of Venice—from 1545 to 1563.
Do they make changes?
Will there still be paintings in the churches?
Contrary to the Protestants' wishes, the council reaffirms the power of images in the Catholic religion.
Artistic creations encourage prayer. . . .
They facilitate learning. . . .
Especially for those who don't know how to read!
After a period of austerity, the popes once again undertake building campaigns in Rome.
What saint are you painting for the Cerasi Chapel?
I'm going to do Saint Paul.
Ah, yes! Saint Paul writing a letter to the Corinthians?
No! Just at the moment of his conversion, when he falls from his horse!
Artists portray dramatic moments in history to stimulate emotion. But from now on, paintings of nudes will not be allowed in churches—not even in the Sistine Chapel.
No more nudes, the pope wants modesty!
Putting clothes on bodies painted by Michelangelo—what a shame!

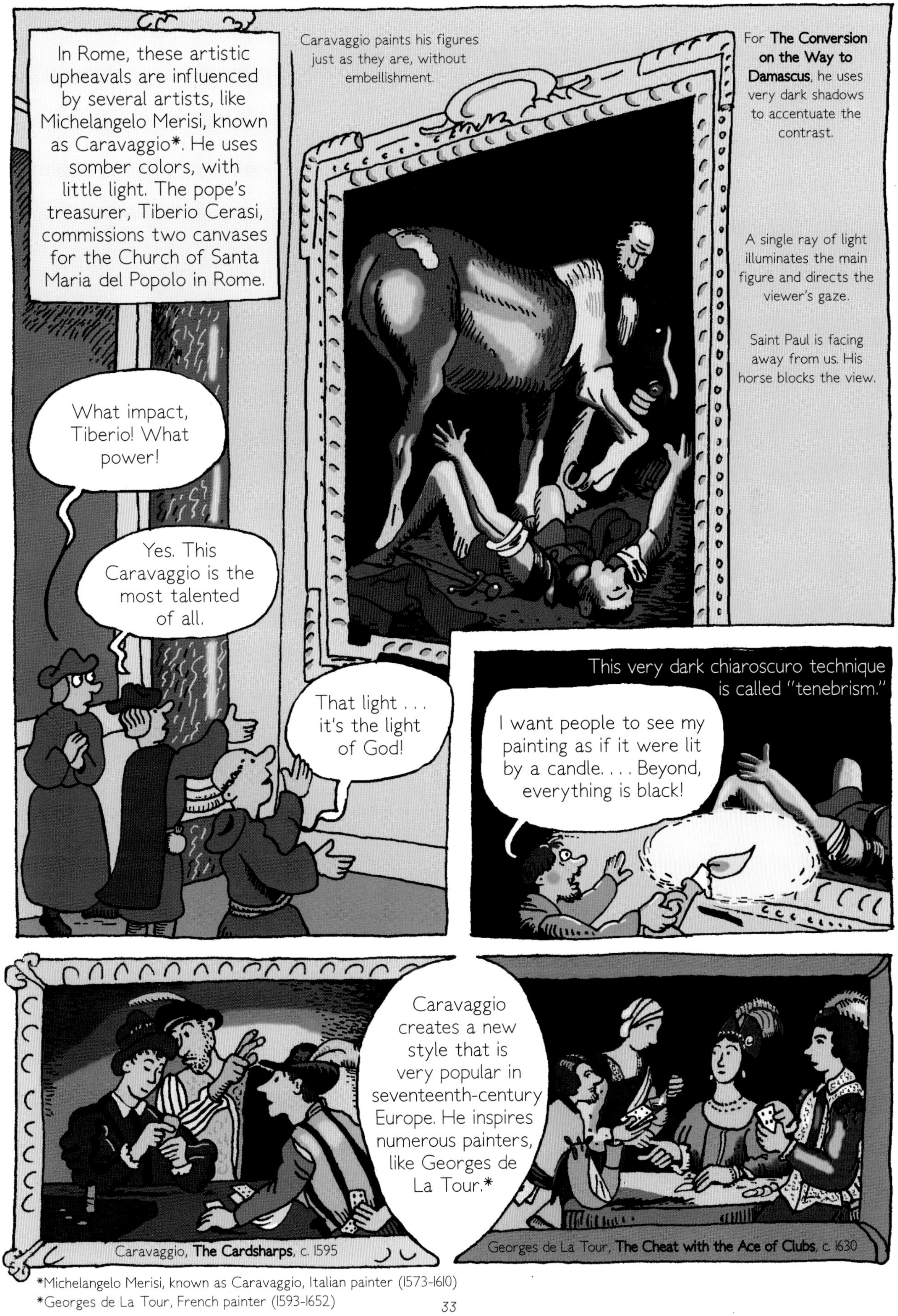

In Rome, these artistic upheavals are influenced by several artists, like Michelangelo Merisi, known as Caravaggio*. He uses somber colors, with little light. The pope's treasurer, Tiberio Cerasi, commissions two canvases for the Church of Santa Maria del Popolo in Rome.
Caravaggio paints his figures just as they are, without embellishment.
For **The Conversion on the Way to Damascus**, he uses very dark shadows to accentuate the contrast.
A single ray of light illuminates the main figure and directs the viewer's gaze.
Saint Paul is facing away from us. His horse blocks the view.
What impact, Tiberio! What power!
Yes. This Caravaggio is the most talented of all.
That light . . . it's the light of God!
This very dark chiaroscuro technique is called "tenebrism."
I want people to see my painting as if it were lit by a candle. . . . Beyond, everything is black!
Caravaggio creates a new style that is very popular in seventeenth-century Europe. He inspires numerous painters, like Georges de La Tour.*
Caravaggio, **The Cardsharps**, c. 1595
Georges de La Tour, **The Cheat with the Ace of Clubs**, c. 1630

*Michelangelo Merisi, known as Caravaggio, Italian painter (1573-1610)
*Georges de La Tour, French painter (1593-1652)

To defend Catholicism after the Council of Trent, the Jesuit priests take charge of teaching in Europe and also in the "new worlds" of Africa, Asia, and the Americas. In 1568 they build the Church of the Gesù in Rome; it will serve as a model for churches throughout the world.

In this church, all of the faithful can see the priest clearly.

If they see, they will believe. . . .

Architecture, sculpture, and painting are influenced by this revival of faith. The style of these churches is called "baroque."

Church of Santa Maria della Salute

Like that church?

Yes.

Baroque architecture is meant to astonish with exaggerated shapes, materials, and colors. The goal is to create unexpected visual effects that evoke an emotion. In 1638 the architect Borromini* builds the Church of San Carlo alle Quattro Fontane in Rome.

The word "baroque" comes from the Portuguese "barroco," which means a pearl of irregular shape.

But, Borromini . . . your wall isn't straight!

It looks like a wave. . . .

My models are the triangle, the ellipse, and the circle! Nature doesn't like straight lines!

*Francesco Borromini, Italian architect (1599-1667)

In 1645, also in Rome, Gian Lorenzo Bernini* decorates a chapel for the wealthy Cornaro family. The principal sculpture shows a woman, Saint Teresa, at the moment when she has a vision of an angel piercing her heart with a golden spear: **The Ecstasy of Saint Teresa**.

Bernini uses several materials: white and colored marble for the figures, and bronze for the rays of golden light.

He "stages" the statue by sculpting balconies with spectators—the Cornaro family—looking at Saint Teresa.

The sculpture seems to be moving! You forget it's made of stone!

And that light—where does that light come from?

A hidden window illuminates the golden rays above Saint Teresa, drawing the viewer's attention.

The saint's body and face are very expressive: eyes half closed, lips parted, hand limp . . . she is in ecstasy, reclining on a cloud.

In the 17th and 18th centuries, baroque art takes hold in Europe. It also spreads to the Spanish and Portuguese colonies in Central and South America. Only France is relatively unaffected by this style.

Church of Saint Francis of Assisi in Ouro Preto, Brazil

*Gian Lorenzo Bernini, Italian sculptor and architect (1598-1680)

In Flanders, young Peter Paul Rubens* is a precociously talented painter. At the age of 23 he leaves Anvers to study the Italian masters. In 1602, he's in Rome.

What light! What life! What power Caravaggio has!

I'll copy this work to absorb its spirit....

Rubens also goes to Madrid, where he studies the collection of paintings owned by the kings of Spain.

Titian is a genius with color!

!

Rubens paints the equestrian portrait of the Duke of Lerma, inspired by Titian's painting of Charles V on horseback.

I'm trying a new composition, a frontal view, as powerful as a Caravaggio and as full of color as a Titian.

Our great King Philip will be pleased!

In 1609, he returns to Anvers. After 40 years of religious conflict, the city is once again at peace. Rubens receives numerous commissions to decorate churches.

I'm going to paint Christ on the cross. But they want a triptych! We're not in the Middle Ages anymore!

You'll manage, Rubens. You know how to do it!

*Peter Paul Rubens, Flemish painter (1577-1640)

The Raising of the Cross is a turning point in Rubens's art. The composition is bursting with life, energy, and emotion, blending the legacy of Flemish painting with that of Italian art.

Jesus's body is muscular and solid. The executioners' muscles are tight.

On the left is a group of weeping women; on the right, soldiers of the Roman army. In the center, the cross bearing Jesus is being raised.

All of the people are in motion and in tension at the same time.

The lighting recalls Caravaggio's chiaroscuro . . .

My painting should dominate us, plunge us into Christ's sacrifice!

. . . and the powerful bodies recall Michelangelo!

Commissions come in from all over Europe. As head of his studio, Rubens is in charge of a flourishing business. In 1621, the Queen of France, Marie de Médici, returns to Paris after a long exile. She commissions a series of 24 large canvases to decorate her new palace.

Rubens, we expect a spectacular job. You are to show my destiny as a wise and farsighted queen!

You have two years! And we want to see all the preliminary sketches.

I shall write your story with my brushes . . .

. . . and also with my imagination.

Rubens also paints large scenes of wild animal hunts. They are popular with European rulers who participate in these hunts.

The Lion Hunt, 1621

Excellency, I have tried to portray the savagery of the fight.

Ah! Interesting diagonal composition!

In the center is a raging lion. Who will win?

In 1628, Rubens is once again in Spain. He becomes friends with the young painter Diego Velázquez*.

My dear Rubens, I am awed by your genius . . . the freedom of your brushwork, your colors . . .

Then go to Italy, Diego. Nourish your talent.

Rubens's studio in Anvers is constantly busy. The master makes small sketches; his assistants transfer them to huge canvases, which Rubens finishes. At the age of 53, he marries a very young woman.

Helena, you are the delight of my old age!

Meanwhile in Madrid, Velazquez is back from Italy and reaching artistic maturity. He is in the service of King Philip IV, a great patron of the arts. He paints the **Portrait of Pablo de Valladolid**, the king's jester.

With you, I'm going to do something different. No background, no wall, no decoration . . . just black, brown, and your shadow to create perspective.

*Diego Velázquez, Spanish painter (1599-1660)

The royal family commissions countless portraits by him.

Master, now we want portraits of the Infanta Margaret, our dear child!

My painting will be sent to the court in Vienna to carry news of the infanta, who is promised in marriage to Emperor Leopold.

In 1656, Velázquez creates his famous portrait of Philip IV's family, **Las Meninas**. In a large room in the palace, the Infanta Margaret is surrounded by maids of honor (meninas), a governess, a bodyguard, two dwarfs, and a dog.

Velázquez shows himself at work on a painting, looking directly at the viewer.

A mirror in the background reflects images of the king and queen—they are the subjects of Velázquez's painting!

My dear Diego, you have created an astonishing work! It invites us into a deep and lifelike scene! What is reality? What is illusion?

In Northern Europe, in the Protestant Low Countries, there are no more religious commissions. On the other hand, well-to-do burghers want to decorate their homes with portraits, landscapes, and scenes of daily life. In 1631, young Rembrandt van Rijn* moves to Amsterdam.

Amsterdam, here I come!

Group portraits are very popular. In 1632, the powerful guild of surgeons gives the young painter a commission.

In a few weeks we'll have the one authorized dissection for this year. We want to commemorate it.

Count on me, I'll be there.

In **The Anatomy Lesson of Dr. Nicolaes Tulp,** Rembrandt manages to paint a scene full of life and intensity despite the seriousness of the subject.

What light! Our faces really stand out!

The painting is a great success. Rembrandt receives numerous commissions.

It's for the entrance hall of our militia headquarters. There will be 18 of us.

Why not show the company in action?

A big painting!

*Rembrandt van Rijn, Dutch painter (1606-1669)

Rembrandt paints a huge canvas showing Captain Frans Banning Cocq's Harquebus militia. It's known as **The Night Watch** because of the way darkness dominates the scene. The artist mixes very precise details with an exaggerated, almost unreal light.

Over the course of his life, Rembrandt makes more than 60 self-portraits, both paintings and engravings! He paints the last one in 1669, shortly before his death. By then he is poor and almost forgotten.

It's not me that I'm painting, it's the passing of time, it's a life....

The brushstrokes are quick, very noticeable, almost rough. The paint is thick, with colors laid over each other to achieve the appearance of skin and fabrics.

A painter in Delft, near Amsterdam, has a special talent for portraying his surroundings: interiors, everyday happenings, and occasionally landscapes. He is Johannes Vermeer*.

What light, Johannes! Everything is glistening after the rain....

Yes, Master Fabritius. I love it when the roofs of our beautiful city sparkle like this....

Vermeer has probably seen canvases by Caravaggio. He also knows Rembrandt's work. He plays with light and shadow to enliven his canvases. And he has something else....

Turn this way.... Look at me.... Don't move! I want to capture that light!

What's that box for, Master?

*Johannes Vermeer, Dutch painter (1632–1675)

Vermeer probably used a camera obscura. It's a simple wooden box with a small hole to let light in. A lens projects an image of the scene onto a slanted mirror at the back of the box.

I can see you on this ground-glass plate—reversed, but very clear. Don't move, I'm going to make a sketch.

During Vermeer's youth, his country is at war. His life is difficult, and he has a large family to feed.

I'm going to go paint where it's quiet. . . .

Thanks to a patron, Vermeer is free to paint familiar, everyday scenes.

In my canvases I try to paint the simple life. Sometimes it seems so far away. . . .

His famous painting **The Milkmaid** (about 1658) is illuminated by soft light from a window.

Vermeer boldly combines bright colors. Blue and yellow, complementary colors, contrast with the white wall at the back of the room.

Tanneke, I'm going to cut off your feet. That will make you seem closer to the viewer.

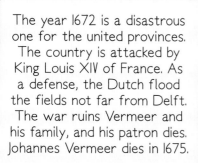

The year 1672 is a disastrous one for the united provinces. The country is attacked by King Louis XIV of France. As a defense, the Dutch flood the fields not far from Delft. The war ruins Vermeer and his family, and his patron dies. Johannes Vermeer dies in 1675.

Louis XIV, the Sun King, enlarges his palace in Paris by building a large façade, the Louvre Colonnade. It's different from baroque architecture; with its straight lines, restraint, and symmetry, it's "French Classicism."

Le Vau, this façade is a triumph. I'm very pleased with it.

Sire, it will show everyone the power and glory of the king!

And protect the palace!

The painter Charles Le Brun* is in charge of decorating the façade. He is also the director of the Royal Academy of Painting.

"Freedom of the arts" is our motto.

Ah! Drawing from a live model . . .

What's an academy?

A sort of school that brings together the best artists in the kingdom.

Are we going back to Paris?

To Versailles!

Louis XIV, an absolute monarch, wants to create a palace that will show the world his power, but one that is also a work of art.

I shall build my palace around my father's small château here at Versailles.

*Charles Le Brun, French painter (1619–1690)

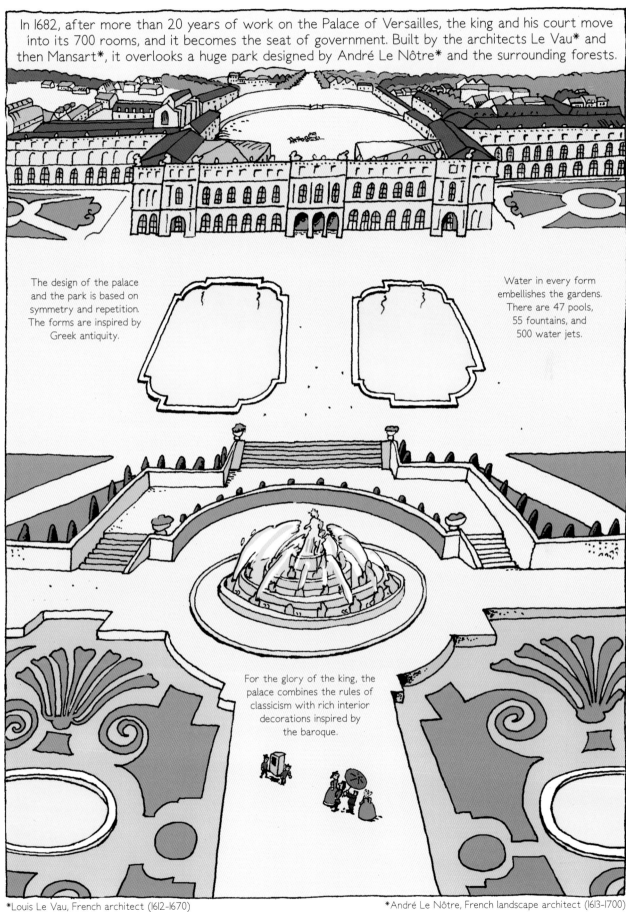

In 1682, after more than 20 years of work on the Palace of Versailles, the king and his court move into its 700 rooms, and it becomes the seat of government. Built by the architects Le Vau* and then Mansart*, it overlooks a huge park designed by André Le Nôtre* and the surrounding forests.

The design of the palace and the park is based on symmetry and repetition. The forms are inspired by Greek antiquity.

Water in every form embellishes the gardens. There are 47 pools, 55 fountains, and 500 water jets.

For the glory of the king, the palace combines the rules of classicism with rich interior decorations inspired by the baroque.

*Louis Le Vau, French architect (1612-1670)

*François Mansart, French architect (1598-1666)

*André Le Nôtre, French landscape architect (1613-1700)

In 1684 the Hall of Mirrors at Versailles is inaugurated. From floor to ceiling, paintings as well as marble and bronze sculptures decorate this huge room dedicated to the glory of the king.

The real painting is on the ceiling: it recounts the history of the kingdom.

Here's the king, who rules alone.

Like an emperor...

Or a god!

The Hall of Mirrors, 240 feet long, is lit by 17 windows; 357 mirrors reflect the setting sun.

Charles Le Brun, who is credited with the ceilings, is the great advocate of classical art. He promotes his ideas through the Academy.

Drawing, always drawing, first of all drawing!

They learn to draw? Not paint?

Both! But artists are constantly debating whether draftsmanship or color is more important.

PARIS

Painting is divided into genres. The most prestigious is historical painting.

HISTOIRE

MYTHOLOGIE

Next comes portrait painting, then scenes of everyday life, then landscapes, animals, and still lifes.

Every month, a painter from the Academy conducts a lesson for his colleagues. Le Brun often chooses to discuss an earlier classicist, Nicolas Poussin*, who lived in Rome.

No exaggerated shadows like with Caravaggio and his followers.

The line is clear and precise. Horizontals, verticals . . .

Les Aveugles de Jéricho
Nicolas Poussin

All of the figures are visible, nothing is hidden.

What a perfect landscape!

At Versailles, many statues grace the huge park. François Girardon* is appointed first sculptor to the king.

Girardon, this statue is magnificent. What power!

My dear Le Brun, I followed your drawings. I also recalled my stay in Rome. . . .

In this sculpture, Pluto steps over another figure as he abducts the nymph Proserpina.

The poses are complex.

They make the viewer want to circle around the work.

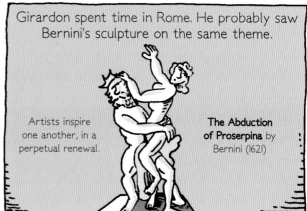

Girardon spent time in Rome. He probably saw Bernini's sculpture on the same theme.

Artists inspire one another, in a perpetual renewal.

The Abduction of Proserpina by Bernini (1621)

*Nicolas Poussin, French painter (1594-1665)
*François Girardon, French sculptor (1628-1715)

Louis XIV dies in 1715. After years of war, the nobles want a life of pleasure and ease.

To Paris! Let the party begin!

Nobles and the well-to-do commission works of art. They like light subjects, rich in curves and colors.

Charming. . . . What style is that?

Rococo! It's new!

These new patrons like scenes of the theater and fashionable entertainments. The painter Antoine Watteau* is a careful observer of the spectacle of Parisian life.

They're performing a comedy, but what sadness in their eyes . . .

In 1717, for admission to the Academy, Watteau presents **Pilgrimage to the Isle of Cythera**. Couples enjoy themselves on their way to this island dedicated to Venus, the goddess of love. Little angels fly around the people.

What is the subject? Dance?

The dance of love and happiness!

You are admitted!

What grace!

*Antoine Watteau, French painter (1684-1721)

48

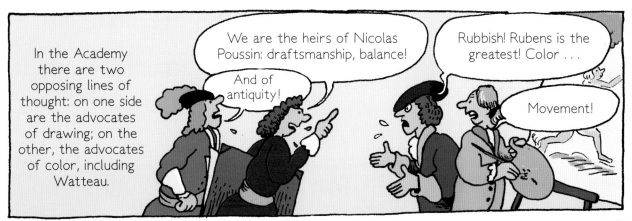

In the Academy there are two opposing lines of thought: on one side are the advocates of drawing; on the other, the advocates of color, including Watteau.

We are the heirs of Nicolas Poussin: draftsmanship, balance!

And of antiquity!

Rubbish! Rubens is the greatest! Color . . .

Movement!

With the new ideas of the Age of Enlightenment, there is less demand for paintings of entertainments. Jean-Baptiste-Siméon Chardin * is an observer of everyday life. Inspired by the Dutch, he paints still lifes, like **The Ray** in 1728.

On the left is life, movement.

On the right, life has been stilled.

What technique!

Look at the materials: the cat's fur, the tablecloth, the reflections in the pot.

And the carcass of the fish . . . the blood . . .

Ewwww!

Yes, we saw that at the Louvre, that bloody fish!

In those days, blood was used much more in cooking.

Gross!

But Chardin also painted children. The **Boy with a Spinning-Top** is playing with a toy instead of studying.

*Jean-Baptiste-Siméon Chardin, French painter (1699-1779)

49

Meanwhile in England, the Industrial Revolution is underway. Londoners are becoming wealthy. To decorate their homes, they, too, appreciate paintings that depict scenes of everyday life.

You'll see, my dear, what a beautiful piece I've brought....

It's a Hogarth, isn't it?

William Hogarth* paints series of works in the Rococo style. In them he criticizes the behavior of his contemporaries.

What's the subject?

Marrying for money.

The paintings in the series **Marriage à-la-Mode** are like six chapters of a story without words.

Ah! The **Tête à Tête**.... What a picture of that couple!

Unfortunately, I can't get it for you. I'll wait until the engravings come out.

Hogarth prints engravings, which are very popular. He becomes a businessman as well as a painter.

He sells his prints, and even advertises.

Hey! A new series from Hogarth, about politics.

I want to see that!

*William Hogarth, English painter and engraver (1697-1764)

The English aristocrats prefer portraits. A number of painters, like Thomas Gainsborough*, specialize in the genre.

I'm having a hard time selling my landscapes.

Well then, Thomas, paint portraits instead. They're in demand!

Portraits are no longer just for the powerful. They have to convey the model's personality.

Frances, I would like to be seen as a gentleman!

Why not you and me as a couple, Robert?

In 1749, Gainsborough paints the portrait **Mr. and Mrs. Andrews**, combining his talent for landscapes with the wishes of the client, who wants to show his marital happiness and his fondness for hunting.

I'll add your portraits next. . . .

He has invented a new style of portraiture.

Très bien!

Rich English people travel to Italy. Like today's tourists, they want to preserve the memory.

What light!

I'll introduce you to a friend who can paint it.

Look at this! I brought these paintings back from Venice. It's such a vibrant city. . . .

Ah, a Canaletto*! I love that artist!

*Thomas Gainsborough, English painter (1727-1788)
*Giovanni Antonio Canal, known as Canaletto, Italian painter (1697-1768)

Italy in the eighteenth century is no longer the center of the art world, but Italian artists are still much in demand throughout Europe. They are called on to decorate baroque churches and new palaces. In 1750, Giovanni Tiepolo* leaves Italy for Würzburg, Germany.

What a huge palace! I'm going to get Domenico to help me.

For three years Tiepolo, with the help of his son, creates splendid frescoes in the Würzburg Palace. In addition to the Imperial Hall, he decorates the vault over the grand staircase.

The theme of the ceiling is Apollo reigning over the four continents.

Tiepolo uses beautiful pastel colors. The trompe-l'oeil decoration includes a host of figures. The illusions are perfect.

As you go up the stair, you discover new scenes!

Father, for Asia should I paint an elephant?

I've added your portrait. Plus several artists that Your Majesty likes. . . .

Ah! That's you there, Tiepolo, I recognize you!

But soon, rich decorations are no longer in fashion. In Europe, especially in France, there are rumblings of revolt against the luxurious lifestyle of the aristocrats.

*Giovanni Battista Tiepolo, Italian painter (1696–1770)

At the beginning of the eighteenth century, ruins are discovered in Italy, near Naples—Herculaneum and Pompeii, buried under ashes from Vesuvius.

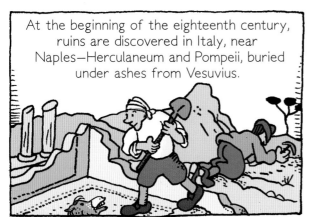

Did you see Pompeii, Hubert?

Yes . . . and I made sketches of the ruins.

It all looks magnificent.

The painter Jacques-Louis David* shares this taste for antiquity. He invents a new style: Neoclassicism.

Enough of the frivolous life! The Enlightenment philosophers were right: We need to return to the moral values of antiquity!

In 1785, David paints the **Oath of the Horatii**, a legend from ancient Rome that has been revived for the classical theater.

I took the subject from Corneille, but it's Poussin who inspired my painting.

David's painting is displayed at the Salon organized in 1785 by the Royal Academy of Painting and Sculpture.

What vigor!

Men ready to die for their country!

Finally! Precise draftsmanship, restraint, pure colors!

I can't see anything, it's too high up!

Beginning in 1735, the Salon Carré (Square Salon) of the Louvre is used regularly to show the works of Academy members. In the 1780s, as many as 1,000 people a day visit the Salon.

*Jacques-Louis David, French painter (1748-1825)

Time Line of the Classical and Modern Periods

1759 British Museum opens in London.

1783 United States of America gains independence.

1789–1799 French Revolution.

1793 Louvre Museum opens in Paris.

1799 The Rosetta Stone is discovered during Napoleon's Egyptian campaign.

1825 First railroad in England is inaugurated.

1830 Paris sees the "Three Glorious Days" of the July Revolution. Eugène Delacroix paints *Liberty Leading the People*.

1839 First mass-produced camera is invented by Louis Daguerre.

1851 Crystal Palace Exhibition is held in London.

1852–1870 Second Empire in France. Major municipal improvements in Paris by Baron Haussmann.

1863 The Academy of Painting holds a Salon in Paris; scandal of Manet's *Olympia*.

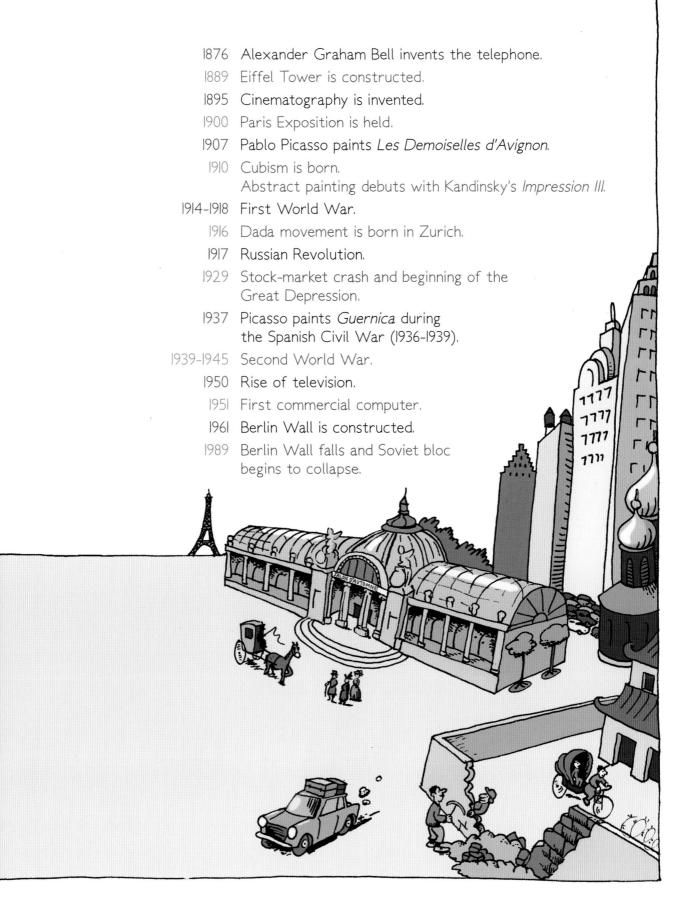

1876   Alexander Graham Bell invents the telephone.

1889   Eiffel Tower is constructed.

1895   Cinematography is invented.

1900   Paris Exposition is held.

1907   Pablo Picasso paints *Les Demoiselles d'Avignon*.

1910   Cubism is born.
Abstract painting debuts with Kandinsky's *Impression III*.

1914-1918   First World War.

1916   Dada movement is born in Zurich.

1917   Russian Revolution.

1929   Stock-market crash and beginning of the
Great Depression.

1937   Picasso paints *Guernica* during
the Spanish Civil War (1936-1939).

1939-1945   Second World War.

1950   Rise of television.

1951   First commercial computer.

1961   Berlin Wall is constructed.

1989   Berlin Wall falls and Soviet bloc
begins to collapse.

On July 14, 1789, revolution comes to Paris! A long period of trouble begins, and is echoed in artists' work.

A hero, ready to die for his ideals!

The Louvre is no longer a royal palace. In 1793 it becomes a public art museum.

I saw the one in London. Fantastic!

Here they only have 660 works.

In 1799, Napoleon Bonaparte and his army leave for Egypt. Dozens of artists accompany him. When they return, the French learn about some of the treasures of Egyptian antiquity.

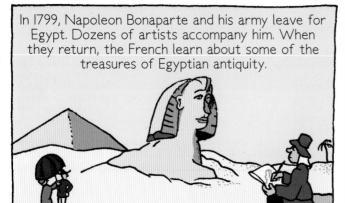

Then Napoleon seizes total power and prepares to have himself crowned Emperor of the French.

David, I like your flawless work. I want a picture for posterity!

Sire, you do me too much honor.

On December 2, 1804, Napoleon is crowned emperor at the Cathedral of Notre Dame, with the pope in attendance. David immortalizes the occasion with an imposing painting. It is a work of propaganda, intended to glorify the emperor and his family.

The Coronation of Napoleon shows the meeting of two worlds: the sacred, on the right, seems to descend upon the secular.

How true to life! It's more than a painting . . . we are alive in this picture!

Our clothes are rendered so well! The fur, the silk, the velvet, the satin of my dress . . .

When Napoleon falls from power in 1815, David flees to Belgium. Jean Dominique Ingres* becomes the leading figure in Neoclassical painting.

What are you painting?

A nude. Inspired by Raphael. What a genius!

Ingres trained at the French Academy in Rome. He was able to see and copy the masterpieces of antiquity and of the Renaissance.

Every year, each student at the Academy in Rome has to send a work to Paris so their progress can be evaluated. In 1808, Ingres chooses to submit his **Valpinçon Bather**. He has a lifelong fascination with the nude female back, which he depicts in several paintings.

The painting is smooth, shadings are light, fabrics are delicately draped. The curtains accentuate the model's graceful curves.

You're going to send a Venus to Paris?

It's not a Venus.

The only subject of my painting is the nude body.

Portraits are what will eventually make Ingres famous . . . in spite of himself. He paints Paris's most elegant women and, in 1832, Louis-François Bertin, the owner of a newspaper.

Cursed portraits! They always keep me from moving on to great things!

Still, you're so gifted. It looks like Mr. Bertin is going to speak . . . or give an order.

You've even painted the reflection of the window on the chair.

*Jean-Auguste-Dominique Ingres, French painter (1780-1867)

In 1808, as Napoleon's power spread across Europe, French troops occupied Spain. Francisco de Goya* had been painter to the King of Spain for almost 20 years. He had become deaf as a result of an illness.

The repression by the French is merciless.... We must denounce it!

Goya paints **The Second of May 1808** and **The Third of May 1808**. These two works show the French soldiers' brutality toward the Spanish population. But Goya is also painting his own rebellion and expressing his feelings. It's the beginning of Romantic painting.

In **The Third of May 1808**, a figure in a white shirt concentrates the light and captures the viewer's attention.

The shadowy background evokes nighttime, but also the darkness of war.

You can sense the painter's gestures, his speed, his energy.

I've tried to use my brush to keep alive the most heroic actions of our brave resistance to the French tyrant!

His emotion, too.

You can see that he has studied Rubens and Velázquez.

*Francisco de Goya, Spanish painter (1746–1828)

Between 1810 and 1815, Goya makes a series of engravings called **The Disasters of War**.

They are not circulated until 1863, after the painter's death.

Should we print these engravings? What they show is absolutely horrible!

Yes, but it's the truth.

In 1819 Goya leaves Madrid, where King Ferdinand VII rules as an absolute monarch. He moves to the countryside.

Here you can rest.

Goya's art bears witness to a period of wars, revolutions, famines . . .

I no longer want to paint beauty, but rather what I feel. It's time for solitude, death, emotion!

On the walls of his house, Goya paints frescoes that are called the **Black Paintings**. They convey a feeling of terrifying mystery, sometimes nightmare.

Colors are limited: ochre, gray, black, and a few whites. The compositions are off-center. Landscapes are drawn with wide brushstrokes.

Are the frescoes still in the house?

No, they were transferred to canvases. You can see them in Madrid, at the Prado Museum.

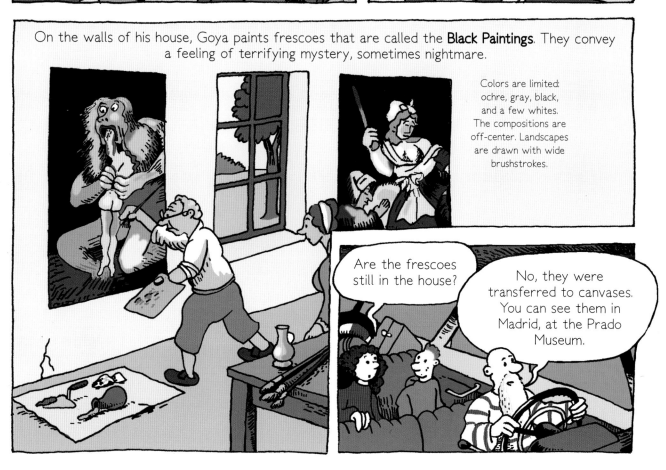

In Paris, the young painter Théodore Géricault* also is interested in current subjects. His 1819 painting **The Raft of the Medusa** is inspired by a tragedy that took place near the coast of Senegal: 147 people adrift at sea on a raft for 13 days after their ship sank.

It's our whole society on that raft....

The terror, the agony, the sorrow...

Théodore, is it an allegory for our country?

That raft is like a human pyramid toppling toward us.

That light and darkness... is there hope, or is this the end?

That pile of corpses... it's disgusting! Not a fit subject for a painting!

It's a triumph! The contemporary is what speaks to the soul!

Ah, the soul, my dear Delacroix...

So were they saved?

No, only 10 survived.

We're coming into Paris!

*Théodore Géricault, French painter (1791–1824)

60

*Eugène Delacroix, French painter (1798-1863)

The painting is bought by Louis Philippe, the new king. But, for fear that it could inspire riots, it is quickly placed in storage.

Romantic art represents a new way of expressing oneself.

Romantic art means modern art, the inner life, spirituality, a yearning for the infinite!

In the middle of the nineteenth century, although Europeans continue to explore the world, they also discover the beauties of nearby nature, and attempt to conquer peaks in the Alps. Caspar David Friedrich* expresses this fascination with untouched spaces in **Wanderer Above the Sea of Fog**.

I am nothing compared to the eternal immensity.

In 1852 Louis-Napoleon Bonaparte, a nephew of Napoleon I, has himself crowned Emperor of the French, taking the name Napoleon III.

Paris is a cesspool. There's a risk of cholera breaking out!

To say nothing of riots in the medieval alleyways!

Napoleon III undertakes huge changes in Paris to make it a modern city. He entrusts the task to Baron Haussmann.

Let's open up the avenues, let's build sewers ... there needs to be air, and light! I want to make Paris at least the equal of London!

Clean up and beautify Paris, that's my mission, sire!

*Caspar David Friedrich, German painter (1774-1840)

In 1855, a World's Fair is organized in France for the first time. It is held in Paris on the Champs-Élysées, and is a huge success.

Five million visitors in six months!

At the fine-arts exhibition, the artists are chosen by members of the Academy.

Here is Liberty guiding the people.

Hmmm.

The art shown at the Salon is called the "official art." In reaction to political and social changes, the "officials" try to revive the artistic forms of the past.

What's happening?

Those are the painters who are furious that they weren't chosen for the Salon.

Gustave Courbet* is furious too. His new work, **The Painter's Studio**, was not selected. In order to display it, he has his own pavilion built, right beside the official one!

What's this?

Bravo for your incredible audacity in appealing directly to the public!

Thank you, my dear Manet!

Courbet admires Géricault and Delacroix. Like them, he chooses to paint large canvases. But rather than episodes from history, he prefers a more familiar world.

Here are the people who come to be painted by me. On the left are the ordinary people, the exploiters . . .

On the right are friends, workers, art lovers . . .

*Gustave Courbet, French painter (1819–1877)

In Paris, many artists meet in cafés—like on Friday evenings at the Café Guerbois.

The artist must live in the very heart of his times.

Of course, but the Louvre is still our school.

Édouard Manet* and other painters copy the old masters at the Louvre.

It's nice, these four people in nature. . . .

Titian

The annual Salon allows painters to show and sell their works. Manet has already been rejected by the Academy several times. But in 1865 . . .

I was inspired by Titian's Venus.

This time, his picture is chosen for exhibit at the Salon. Manet's **Olympia** creates a huge scandal.

It's badly painted!

It's not a goddess, just a naked woman!

Exactly! A courtesan, I'd say!

Besides, she's proud of herself. . . . She's looking at us. What a disgrace!

Olympia of the streets, maybe!

*Édouard Manet, French painter (1832–1883)

Despite the support of his writer and poet friends, Manet is dejected.

You are the painter of modern life.

The present times are worthy of the brush. Hang in there!

Several painters around Manet reject the Academy's rules: Monet, Degas, Renoir . . .

Let's go to the country. I want to paint from nature.

No way! Me, I'll paint the city.

I'll come with you to Argenteuil.

In 1859, paint becomes available in tubes with caps. The ready-mixed colors can be carried anywhere.

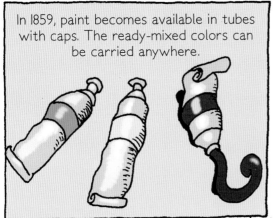

Thanks to this innovation, painters take their folding easels and leave the studio.

We need to work quick, the color of the water is constantly changing!

In 1870, during the Franco-Prussian War, Paris is a combat zone. Some painters stay. Others, like Claude Monet and Camille Pissarro, leave for London. There, they discover the works of English painters—Constable* and especially Turner*.

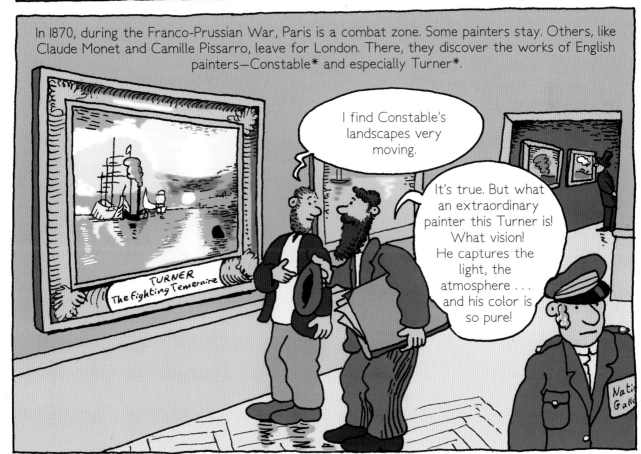

I find Constable's landscapes very moving.

It's true. But what an extraordinary painter this Turner is! What vision! He captures the light, the atmosphere . . . and his color is so pure!

TURNER
The Fighting Temeraire

*John Constable, English painter (1776-1837)
*J. M. W. Turner, English painter (1775-1851)

65

At the end of his life, William Turner paints dream versions of landscape scenes. The subject blurs, becoming movement and color.

Snow, wind, rain . . . and LIGHT!

In **Snow Storm: Steam-Boat off a Harbour's Mouth** (1842) the steamboat disappears in the storm. All that remains are white and blue streaks that create movement.

Turner is initially influenced by Romantic landscapes like those of Friedrich.

Manet, very impressed by Turner's techniques, returns to his friends in Paris.

Join us, Manet. We want to exhibit together!

No, my friends, I want to be recognized by the Salon!

About 1840, photography is invented. It's revolutionary; a photo records reality more faithfully and more quickly than a painting. A number of studios open; the most famous one in Paris is Nadar's*.

Look at me, my dear Miss Bernhardt, and above all don't move!

*Gaspard-Félix Tournachon, known as Nadar, French photographer (1820-1910)

*Eugène Boudin, French painter (1824–1898)
*Alfred Sisley, English-French painter (1839–1899)

EUSK

*Berthe Morisot, French painter (1841–1895)
*Claude Monet, French painter (1840–1926)

Look! A train station!

If the car is broken down, can we take the train?

It used to be a train station. Now it's the Orsay Museum. Let's go take a look while we wait for the mechanic. We'll see another train station . . .

. . . the Gare Saint-Lazare, a painting by Monet!

That's weird, painting a train station!

Trains, stations, smoke—they all were subjects for the Impressionists.

The Monet family lives at Argenteuil, in the countryside but easily accessible by train. Monet often passes through the Gare Saint-Lazare, and he paints it a dozen times, at different hours of the day.

Tell the fireman to get the steam up!

Yes, Mr. Claude.

Auguste Renoir* sets up his easel in the cafés and ballrooms where Parisians eat, drink, and dance on Sundays.

I want to capture the movement of the dancers. A painting should be pleasing, cheerful, and pretty. Yes, pretty!

He often paints scenes of pleasure outings. He emphasizes the people, especially the women.

What are those spots?

That's light flickering through the leaves. Renoir is a master at showing such contrasts.

*Auguste Renoir, French painter (1841-1919)

Other Impressionist painters, like Edgar Degas*, are happy to embrace photography. It lets them envision new ways of framing their pictures.

Let's not move now, my friends. Degas is going to immortalize our orchestra.

Look at me, gentlemen!

In 1889, a World's Fair is held in Paris. In June of that year, Claude Monet exhibits with the famous sculptor Auguste Rodin*. For the painter, who has spent years in poverty, this is the beginning of his art being recognized.

Rodin is inspired by the sculpture of antiquity and by Michelangelo's expressiveness. **The Thinker** is first titled The Poet. It represents Dante, author of the Divine Comedy.

This is my **Thinker**. . . . If I could only keep one sculpture, it would be this one!

Keep them all, dear fellow! What expressive power!

But at the same time, these wonderful sculptures could overshadow my paintings.

Unlike his predecessors, Rodin is not interested in idealized forms. He opens the way for modern sculpture.

Hmm. . . . Is it finished?

I never know when it's finished!

*Edgar Degas, French painter (1834-1917
*Auguste Rodin, French sculptor (1840-1917)

The economy is thriving, and the art market is changing. Painters become independent artists, selling their pictures to buyers called "art dealers." To find purchasers, they have to show their works. It's a difficult task for artists who are not well known.

I'll sell them, you'll see!

Claude Monet, now living in Normandy, creates a world of plants and water in his garden at Giverny. The water lilies in his pond are an inexhaustible source of inspiration.

No ground, no horizon . . . The viewer will be facing the surface of water all around, with no reference points—no up, no down, no right, no left. . . .

Monet finishes his canvases in his studio, applying multiple layers. The paint is thick and heavily worked.

After the painter's death in 1927, eight large panels of his water lilies are installed in the Orangerie Museum in Paris. This unique masterwork foreshadows the art of the future.

Paul Cézanne*, a companion of the Impressionists at the beginning, works on his own in Aix-en-Provence. He opens the way for a totally new kind of painting. His favorite subject is the nearby Mont Sainte-Victoire. During his lifetime he paints it nearly 80 times!

I don't see objects—not the mountain or the fields. I see triangles, circles, rectangles. The shape is what interests me!

Cézanne tries to "impose order" in his landscapes. He begins his canvases outdoors and completes them at home.

I'll go back and finish in the studio.

Cézanne paints numerous still lifes. He assembles flowers, fruits, and other objects; studies their volumes; and chooses colors to create a collection of shapes.

Hortense? Are there any more apples?

I want people to sense that my objects are heavy, solid. When the color is at its most powerful, the shape is at its fullest!

Are you finished? Can I take the apples for my pie?

*Paul Cézanne, French painter (1839-1906)

Cézanne wants to paint the underlying anatomy, or structure, of the landscape. This approach will influence several generations of artists.

Time and reflection slowly change our vision. . . . Then understanding comes.

Vincent van Gogh* comes from Holland to work in Provence. He stops first in Paris, in 1886, to see his brother Theo.

Theo, I have so much to learn. . . .

Vincent, you'll find that here in Paris, where everything is happening.

In Paris, van Gogh discovers Impressionist painting and meets many artists. His canvases become more luminous, their colors brighter.

What do we see? Spots of color that the eye combines. . . .

I understand, my dear Signac*. Colors that complement each other . . .

Van Gogh also admires Japanese prints, which he discovers in Paris.

What's this?

A Japanese print. I got it at Bing's*.

Ill at ease in Paris, van Gogh goes to paint at Arles, in Provence.

What light! What a peaceful place! I'd like to create an artists community here.

The Yellow House (1888)

*Vincent van Gogh, Dutch painter (1853-1890)
*Paul Signac, French Neo-Impressionist painter (1863-1935)
*Samuel Siegfried Bing, Parisian art dealer (1838-1905)

The painter Paul Gauguin* joins van Gogh in Provence. The two men admire each other, but they can't get along.

I want to make paintings outdoors, for everyone!

Me, I'm going back to the studio.

Penniless, alone, and suffering from hallucinations, van Gogh paints numerous self-portraits. His pictures reflect his inner life. The paint is thick, with swirling brushstrokes.

Paul Gauguin decides to look for inspiration very far from France, in Tahiti and the other islands of the Pacific. He paints mysterious scenes in intense colors.

In my paintings I seek the truth of a simple life. I'm leaving to find it somewhere else, in a world that's still intact.

*Paul Gauguin, French painter (1848-1903)

In **The Starry Night**, van Gogh paints what he sees, but also what he imagines. The large yellow circle is Venus, which is particularly bright on this night. The painter adds an imaginary church and strange movements in the sky to create a scene that is mysterious and profound.

What art needs today is for a work to be violently vivid, highly colored, and dazzlingly executed!

At the salon in the fall of 1905, Henri Matisse* shows a portrait that is soon famous.

So, my dear, did you see beautiful things?

It's all crazy!

Woman with a Hat is a classic portrait: a woman dressed in middle-class fashion and wearing an elegant hat looks back at the viewer. But Matisse not only uses bright colors, he uses them in unreal ways: a green face, bright red hair, a background made up of flat patches of color.

If you ask me, these Fauvists are a bunch of wild animals!

A green face?

It's just crude dabbling.

It's a pot of paint thrown in the face of the public!

*Henri Matisse, French painter (1869-1954)

Matisse and his "wild" friends, the Fauves, follow the paths blazed by Cézanne, Gauguin, and van Gogh.

At the dawn of the twentieth century, Paris is the artistic capital of Europe. The Norwegian Edvard Munch* has been working there since 1889.

The camera can't compete with the brush. How can you take a photograph of heaven or hell?

Back in Norway, Munch pushes van Gogh's approach even further. In **The Scream**, he presents a vision that challenges all of our perceptions. It's the beginning of a new movement called "Expressionism."

All the lines seem to come from a single point: the mouth of the person in the foreground.

Is it the person that's screaming? Or are they covering their ears against a scream from outside?

I was walking on a path beside a fjord. . . . Suddenly the sky turned blood red!

I stopped. . . . I sensed an infinite scream passing through the universe and ripping nature apart.

In Germany, too, young painters object to the official art. In Munich, they form a group called "The Blue Rider."

Let us seek in nature that which is hidden behind the veil of appearances.

Blue is the male principle, stern and spiritual. Yellow is feminine, soft and happy. Red is brutish.

*Edvard Munch, Norwegian painter (1863-1944)

In Munich, the 30-year-old Russian Wassily Kandinsky* joins The Blue Rider. He is a painter but also an art theorist. He publishes books arguing that authentic art is inseparable from a spiritual process.

Goodbye to landscapes and portraits. Art should express our inner visions!

Kandinsky and the artists of The Blue Rider want to establish connections between painting and music, which they believe can directly express the feelings of the human soul. For them, painting no longer "represents" anything real—it is abstract.

This is my **Composition VII**! Colors are music, music is emotion, art is thought.

Can you hear the colors vibrating?

*Wassily Kandinsky, Russian painter (1866-1944)

In Paris, too, artists are connecting with each other. Several work in Montmartre. In 1905, a young painter from Barcelona moves there.

I'm Pablo Picasso*. Nice to meet you.

My name is Apollinaire. I'm a poet. Welcome to the neighborhood, Pablo.

They are enthusiastic about the works of Cézanne and the Fauvists, and continue their investigations.

Come on, Braque, let's go to Vollard's.* He's showing Cézanne.

I'll be right with you, Pablo.

Cézanne is a master. He is reinventing painting.

In London, André Derain* discovers the art of faraway continents—Africa, Oceania . . .

This is pure art, the art of the first humans!

Inspired by these discoveries, in 1907 Picasso paints **Les Demoiselles d'Avignon**. The picture is astonishing in its impact and its novelty.

The distorted bodies are drawn with sharp edges and from several angles. Viewers lose their bearings.

Revolutionary!

A page has been turned!

Who are these ladies behind their masks?

*Pablo Picasso, Spanish painter (1881-1973)
*Ambrose Vollard, Parisian art dealer (1866-1939)
*André Derain, French painter (1880-1954)

Pablo Picasso and Georges Braque* work together. They draw everyday objects as seen from several angles at the same time, splintered into multiple facets. The objects are broken up and reassembled to create a new way of seeing. It's the birth of Cubism.

Look, Pablo, this time I made a painting of a collage.

That's genius, it looks so real!

In **Fruit Dish, Ace of Clubs**, Braque limits his colors to black, gray, brown, and white.

In Montmartre, young Marcel Duchamp* is interested in scientific progress and technical innovations. He looks to them for new sources of inspiration.

Duchamp, painting no longer has a subject, just shapes and colors!

Me, I want to paint movement, speed!

In 1912, in Munich, Duchamp discovers the paintings of The Blue Rider. Back in Paris, he abandons canvases and instead produces enigmatic works that combine painting and sculpture.

We're seeing a revolution in science: X-rays show what is within matter. Painting should show the invisible within the visible.

*Georges Braque, French painter (1882-1963)
*Marcel Duchamp, French artist (1887-1968)

In 1917, Duchamp goes further: he decides to choose and sign an object, then have it exhibited in a salon. His provocative entry, an inverted urinal, is not displayed to the public.

I'll bet that by taking one of these commonplace objects, and signing it and dating it, I can turn it into an art object!

Three days to repair the car?

What are we going to do?

We're going to see something else mechanical— the Pompidou!

Duchamp makes his choice and opens a new era. It's no longer the production of an object that makes a work of art, but simply the idea, the intellectual process.

With Duchamp, art is reflection. . . . He transforms everyday objects into artworks. His **Readymades** represent choices by the artist.

R.MUTT 1917

From 1916 to 1918, Europe is ripped apart by war. In the face of such horror, artists take refuge in humor and in the imaginary.

Choose provocation!

A huge practical joke!

In Switzerland, in Germany, and soon in Paris and New York, they form the Dada movement.

DADAAAAEIOO !

UUU !

With the end of the war, Paris is once again at the center of the new artistic currents.

Dada soirée this evening at the festival hall!

Dada or not, you'll leave gaga!

The Dada artists see themselves as clever and cheeky. They make fun of the "antiquated values" of the past.

Mona Lisa's smile annoys me. . . .

What if I gave her a little mustache?

The poet André Breton discovers Dada paintings, collages, and objects. For him, they open the doors of the imagination and of dreams. He is fascinated by the work of the Italian Giorgio de Chirico*.

What an enigma! De Chirico paints our dreams. . . .

Dada doesn't last, but it has scattered its seeds. Many artists want to challenge a hypocritical and self-centered society.

We want to change life.

Liberate the imaginary!

The Austrian physician Sigmund Freud has developed psychoanalysis, a treatment method based on exploring the subconscious.

Tell me your dreams. . . .

I see a house on fire and someone flying through the air. . . .

For the "Surrealist" artists, these unconscious visions are a huge reservoir of experiences and a way to achieve freedom. They play artistic games, manipulating objects, texts, drawings, collages, photographs . . .

A corpse . . .

Exquisite!

*Giorgio de Chirico, Italian painter (1888–1978)

Their first exhibition is held in Paris in 1925. Others follow in London and New York, featuring the Spaniard Salvador Dali*, the American Man Ray*, the German Max Ernst*, and the Belgian René Magritte*.

Soft watches, Dali? Are they melting?

Not at all! It's simply **The Persistence of Memory**!

A world of symbols.

According to the Surrealists, a word should not be confused with an image, nor an object with its depiction.

Weird . . .

By golly, that's a pipe, no matter what it says!

Ceci n'est pas une pipe

Other artists follow the paths opened by Cubism and Kandinsky. In the Netherlands, Piet Mondrian* paints geometric shapes in primary colors.

Farewell to figures! I'm trying to find universal harmony with lines, right angles, and color!

*Salvador Dalí, Spanish painter (1904-1989)
*Emmanuel Radnitzky, known as Man Ray, American artist (1890-1976)
*Max Ernst, German Artist (1891-1976)

*René Magritte, Belgian painter (1898-1967)
*Piet Mondrian, Dutch painter (1872-1944)

During the Second World War, European artists take refuge in the United States. New York becomes the center of artistic life. In 1939, the Museum of Modern Art exhibits the monumental work **Guernica** painted two years earlier by Picasso.

Guernica! What incredible power!

It's a twentieth-century **Massacre of the Innocents**!

After the war, New York continues to attract artists. Jackson Pollock* is influenced by Picasso and the Surrealists. Beginning in 1967, he uses a totally new technique: action or "gestural" painting, in which the artist moves around and over the canvas.

When I paint, I feel as if I'm living on the canvas, barely aware of what I'm doing. A painting has a life of its own, and I try to let it come through.

Pollock uses regular house paint. The whole canvas is painted the same way; there is no center. This is called "all-over composition."

Captivated by this lively painting, some artists create "performances": works of art that are short-lived and participatory.

?

Others look for inspiration in everyday objects. They recycle the castoffs of consumer society.

Hey, a tire!

An old blanket!

*Jackson Pollock, American painter (1912-1956)

Then comes the birth of Pop Art ("pop" as in "popular"). Artists like Jasper Johns* adopt the symbols of American identity.

Seven red stripes, six white, and 48 stars . . .

Others, like Roy Lichtenstein*, find inspiration in advertising and comic strips.

OHHH... ALRIGHT...

Andy Warhol*, a young commercial illustrator in New York, paints series of works depicting canned goods, banknotes, Coca-Cola bottles, and movie actresses.

Marilyn Monroe is a consumer product. Her image no longer belongs to her. But is it art?

INK

TOMATO SOUP

SOUP

Silk-screen printing, invented in China in the eighth century, is a way to make reproductions using stencils. Images can be transferred to different materials: cloth, paper, glass, metal . . .

An overlay of the image is placed on a screen coated with a light-sensitive emulsion.

The unexposed areas of emulsion wash away, so ink can go through the screen.

Ink passes through the screen and is deposited on the material.

*Jasper Johns, American artist (b. 1930)
*Roy Lichtenstein, American artist (1923-1997)

*Andy Warhol, American artist (1928-1987)

Beginning in the 1970s, artists adopt new materials and means of expression. They use photos and videos, and they create "installations" in which the spectators are invited to come in and walk around.

We can be INSIDE the work of art!

Not me, I'm afraid of spiders!

Maman (1999), bronze sculpture by Louise Bourgeois*

Drawing, painting, and sculpture are still the preferred means of expression. The Englishman Francis Bacon* paints figures, often nude, that seem to be suffering.

It's figurative, but . . .

The elements are recognizable, but distorted. . . .

The surroundings are undefined. A familiar nowhere.

In New York in the 1980s, young artists like Keith Haring* and Jean-Michel Basquiat* take to the streets.

Graffiti becomes painting, painting becomes graffiti.

I've seen that somewhere.

On the street . . .

. . . or in the subway?

It's the beginning of street art—art of the streets and public spaces. It can be graffiti, tags, posters, stencils, wall paintings, wrapped monuments, lighting installations, video projections . . .

I see one on that chimney over there!

*Louise Bourgeois, French-American artist (1911–2010)
*Francis Bacon, English painter (1909–1992)

*Keith Haring, American artist (1958–1990)
*Jean-Michel Basquiat, American artist (1960–1988)

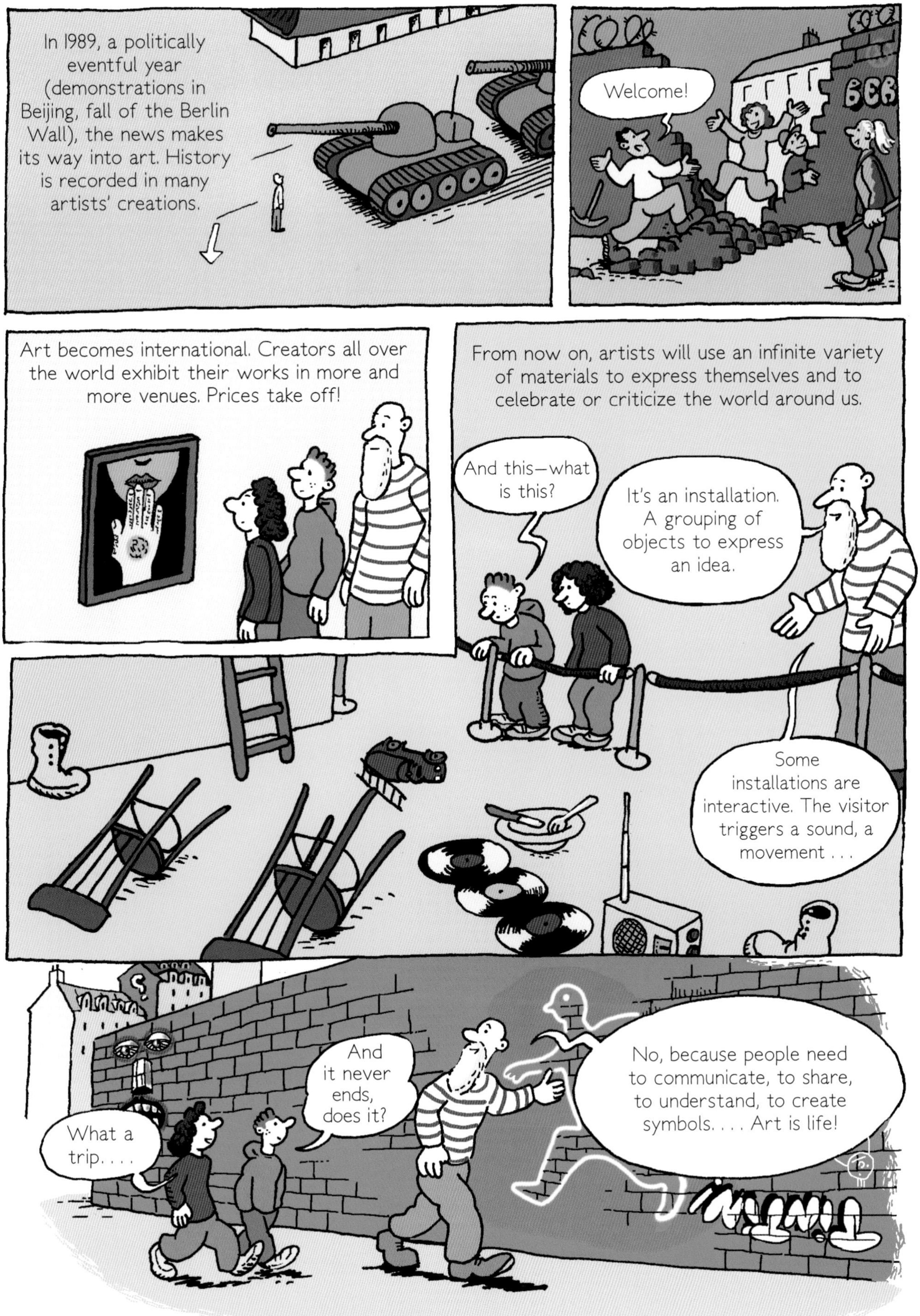
In 1989, a politically eventful year (demonstrations in Beijing, fall of the Berlin Wall), the news makes its way into art. History is recorded in many artists' creations.
Welcome!
Art becomes international. Creators all over the world exhibit their works in more and more venues. Prices take off!
From now on, artists will use an infinite variety of materials to express themselves and to celebrate or criticize the world around us.
And this—what is this?
It's an installation. A grouping of objects to express an idea.
Some installations are interactive. The visitor triggers a sound, a movement . . .
What a trip. . . .
And it never ends, does it?
No, because people need to communicate, to share, to understand, to create symbols. . . . Art is life!

The Art of the Renaissance

The Last Supper by Leonardo da Vinci

The Last Supper is a very large mural painted in the refectory, or dining hall, at the Convent of Santa Maria delle Grazie in Milan, Italy. It shows Jesus, surrounded by his disciples, at his last meal before he was arrested. Leonardo painted it in 1498 on dry plaster, which unfortunately did not hold up well, and today this masterpiece is badly deteriorated.

Portrait of Baldassare Castiglione by Raphael

Painted around 1514 or 1515, this is a portrait of the painter's friend Baldassare Castiglione. Raffaello Sanzio, known as Raphael, conveys the model's strong but natural, unpretentious bearing in shades of gray, black, and white. The painting can be seen at the Louvre in Paris.

Moses by Michelangelo Buonarroti

Michelangelo sculpted this imposing white marble statue of Moses in 1513 for the tomb of Pope Julius II. The stern-faced prophet is seated, his body tense, his powerful muscles ready to move. The sculpture is housed in the church of San Pietro in Vincoli in Rome

The Tempest by Giorgione

Painted about 1507 by the Venetian artist Giorgione da Castelfranco, *The Tempest* is a mysterious, intensely colored work. For the first time in Renaissance art, the landscape is unmistakably the subject, almost relegating the people to secondary status. It can be seen at the Gallerie dell'Accademia in Venice.

Portrait of the Artist Holding a Thistle by Albrecht Dürer

Painted about 1493, when he was twenty-two years old, this self-portrait was created by Albrecht Dürer at the end of his apprenticeship. It is one of the first self-portraits in Western painting. It is on exhibit at the Louvre in Paris.

The Garden of Earthly Delights (detail) by Hieronymus Bosch

The Garden of Earthly Delights is a triptych by the Flemish artist Hieronymus Bosch. Painted in oil on wood between 1490 and 1500, it shows the painter's vision of paradise on earth. It is complex and enigmatic, with a host of curious and fantastic details meticulously painted. It is on display at the Museo del Prado in Madrid.

The Art of the Baroque and Classical Eras

The Judgement of Paris
by Peter Paul Rubens

Painted by the Flemish artist Peter Paul Rubens around 1635, *The Judgement of Paris* shows the young shepherd, accompanied by the god Mercury, judging the beauty of three nude goddesses, Venus, Juno, and Minerva. The large painting, filled with color and movement, highlights the female form. It can be seen at the National Gallery in London.

Las Meninas
by Diego Velázquez

In this 1656 painting, the Spanish artist Diego Velázquez shows Maria Theresa, the daughter of Spain's King Philip IV, surrounded by servants in a room at the palace in Madrid. The painter included himself, brush in his hand, with his eyes fixed on the viewer. What does the painting mean? It's a mystery. The work can be seen at the Museo del Prado in Madrid.

Apollo and Daphne
by Gian Lorenzo Bernini

The Italian artist Bernini sculpted *Apollo and Daphne* between 1622 and 1625. The 8-foot-tall marble shows the nymph Daphne transforming into a laurel tree in order to escape from Apollo. Bernini imparts a light, twirling movement to the couple. The sculpture can be seen in the Galleria Borghese in Rome.

David with the Head of Goliath
by Michelangelo Merisi, called Caravaggio

Around 1607 Caravaggio painted a young David who has just cut off the head of the giant Goliath. Using chiaroscuro, and a light source from one side only, the artist draws the viewer's gaze to the scene's dramatic elements: the sword, David's arm, Goliath's face. The painting is on exhibit at the Galleria Borghese in Rome.

Girl with a Pearl Earring
by Johannes Vermeer

This work was painted by Johannes Vermeer about 1665 in Delft, in the Netherlands. A young girl's face is turned toward the viewer. Framed in a harmonious combination of yellows and blues, it stands out against the dark background, the soft light playing on her fair skin. The painting is in the Mauritshuis in The Hague, Netherlands..

Self-Portrait as the Apostle Paul
by Rembrandt van Rijn

The Dutch painter Rembrandt van Rijn painted this self-portrait at the age of fifty-five. His lined face emerges from the darkness; his white turban and the pages of a book catch the light. At the left, beside the saint's right shoulder, Rembrandt wrote his name and the year of the painting: 1661. This work is on exhibit at the Rijksmuseum in Amsterdam.

The Art of the 18th and 19th Centuries

Pilgrimage to the Isle of Cythera
by Antoine Watteau

The French painter Antoine Watteau created the large composition *Pilgrimage to the Isle of Cythera* between 1712 and 1717. He invented a new genre of painting, the "fête galante," mixing the mythological with the contemporary. In this imaginary scene, couples embrace as they make their way to Cythera, the Island of Love. The painting is on display at the Louvre in Paris.

Portrait of Louis-François Bertin
by Jean-Auguste-Dominique Ingres

In 1832 the French painter Jean-Auguste-Dominique Ingres made this portrait of a sixty-year-old man, his body tense and his expression commanding, looking intently at the viewer. The realism of the *Portrait of Louis-François Bertin*, with its precise details and close framing, made it a model depiction of a prosperous businessman of the period. The painting is in the Louvre in Paris.

The Parasol
by Francisco de Goya

This oil on linen is a study for a tapestry that would have hung above a window in the palace in Madrid. With a colorful play of light and shadow, it is part of a 1777 series that was Francisco de Goya's first success. It is in the Museo del Prado in Madrid.

The Raft of the Medusa
by Théodore Géricault

The Raft of the Medusa by Théodore Géricault was the highlight of the Academy of Painting's 1819 Salon in Paris. Inspired by the accounts of two survivors of a shipwreck, the painter created a huge, tragic scene in dark tones. Today the work is on display at the Louvre in Paris.

The Balcony
by Édouard Manet

In 1868-1869, Édouard Manet painted this scene of middle-class life of the period. But everything about it disturbed his contemporaries: the bright colors, particularly the green of the balcony; the facial expressions that seem lost in thought; the stiff poses. The work is on display at the Musée d'Orsay in Paris.

The Thinker
by Auguste Rodin

Auguste Rodin's most famous sculpture was conceived of in 1880. The original, in plaster, measures 28 inches tall. Numerous castings of the sculpture exist, many of them larger than the original. The definitive version of the sculpture is in bronze and was cast in 1904. It can be seen at the Musée Rodin in Paris.

.. ... to the Art of Today . ....

Dance at Le Moulin de la Galette
by Auguste Renoir

In *Dance at Le Moulin de la Galette*, the French painter Auguste Renoir captures the atmosphere of the cabarets in Paris's Montmartre district. The light, the bright colors, the blurred shapes of dancing couples, the orchestra . . . everything suggests gaiety and movement. Renoir presented the work at the Impressionist Exhibition of 1877. The painting is now on display at the Musée d'Orsay in Paris.

Mont Sainte-Victoire
by Paul Cézanne

Between about 1885 and 1905 Paul Cézanne painted this landscape in Provence, France, many times, rendering it as a series of lines and geometric shapes. Adjacent brushstrokes create first shadow, then light. His paintings of Mont Sainte-Victoire can be seen in numerous museums; this one is on display at the Hermitage Museum in Saint Petersburg, Russia.

Self-Portrait
by Vincent van Gogh

This 1889 self-portrait, one of at least thirty-five by Vincent van Gogh, shows the Dutch painter in a turquoise-blue jacket against a background of the same color enlivened by bluish swirls. In contrast, his orange-toned face and his expression draw the viewer's attention. The bright colors and visible brushstrokes create an atmosphere of tension. The canvas is on display at the Musée d'Orsay in Paris.

Composition VII by Wassily Kandinsky

Composition VII is a huge oil painting by the Russian artist Wassily Kandinsky. Painted in 1913 in Munich, the work is all in motion, depicting a world of color where shapes are no longer identifiable. The title emphasizes its similarity to a piece of music. It marks the birth of abstraction in art. It is on display at the Tretyakov Gallery in Moscow.

Composition in Red, Yellow, Blue, and Black by Piet Mondrian

This work by Piet Mondrian from 1921 is in a style—neoplasticism—the artist invented in an effort to free painting from mere imitation by reducing nature to its essentials: vertical and horizontal lines. In his compositions, Mondrian relies on the golden ratio, the ideal proportion of the ancient Greeks. This painting is in the Municipal Museum of the Hague in the Netherlands.

INDEX